I0134366

Truth in the Flesh

Introducing Apologetics to the Local Church

John G. Hartung

Truth in the Flesh

Copyright © 2012 by John G. Hartung

Cover Design by Bill Finch

Published by: Theocentric Publishing Group
                         1069 Main Street
                         Chipley, Florida 32428
                         http://www.theocentricpublishing.com

All rights reserved. No part of this book may be reproduced or transmitted in any form or by any means without written permission of the author.

Library of Congress Control Number: 2012943729

ISBN 9780985618117

In fond memory of

Dr. Knox Chamblin

December 28, 1935 – February 7, 2012

And

Dr. Walter Wynn Kenyon

February 12, 1948 – February 13, 2012

"You have many teachers in the Lord, but not many fathers."

Foreword

THE AGNOSTIC'S PRAYER

I have seen more than one piece on the internet giving substantial objections to the use of the "Sinner's prayer" in evangelism. Myself, I have led someone to Christ using the Agnostic's prayer.

The prayer is valuable for intelligent friends who are sensitive to the sources of skepticism that are so much part of the modern plausibility structure. I present an apologetic witness, using arguments for theism and criticisms of naturalism. But my presumption is that these are of some value to those whose conscience won't allow them to consider faith due to an inadequate and incomplete picture of the philosophical case for theism. My aim is to bring them to the point where their desire for meaning is peaked and where a theistic interpretation of life seems again like a live option.

There is a way one can get stuck here because of caution. That's when I suggest the Agnostic's prayer:

"Dear God, if there is a God, save my soul, if I have a soul."

On the one hand, praying this prayer is a reasonable risk if one cannot rule out the possibility that a good God exists who saw to it that human beings exist with inherently religious dispositions. But it is also a commitment to be prepared to accept evidence for answered prayer according to the proportion of what we are able to know.

This prayer assumes that not all demands for evidence are legitimate. Bertrand Russell famously said that if he died and stood before the Seat of Judgment and God asked him why he did not believe, that Russell would say, "There was not enough evidence". But Russell had a narrow view of what was possible for humans to know. If someone wants proof that he or she is not wired into the Matrix, it may not be forthcoming. Or if they will accept only scientifically supported generalizations, the organ may essentially not be suited to the purpose. And this could be that God could not provide such evidence of Himself, divine nature and human nature being what they essentially are. To overcome such skepticism would be to change someone from being a human into a being God-like omniscient being. And this is not logically possible for a human. No one, including God, could be obliged to do the logically impossible. So the demand for such evidence is illegitimate.

But on the other hand, it is clear that humans have an insatiable desire to understand and phenomenological evidence of cognitive activity that gathers evidence, forms hypotheses, judges their truth, and assumes responsibility for doing so. We also have a richer array of belief-forming processes such as the immediate knowledge of the first principles of demonstration and explanation and truths we cannot not know, as well as the general reliability of the senses, memory, deduction, induction, and credible testimony. If God exists then we expect that these cognitive processes are as good as what they appear to be. So if God exists, we expect Him to adapt His message to this truth seeking design. If we pray the agnostic's prayer, we are prepared to act on what evidence God may give us. So if these are reliable then maybe there is enough evidence after all. But if one denies the reliability of these processes then they are that way by nature and God cannot be obliged to meet the demand for evidence apart from them. In that case, God can still hold us responsible for not making a reasonable gamble by betting on His existence.

The Agnostic's prayer is a kind of promise making. It is open to possibilities that may or may not obtain, but because it is a promise it brings about a state of affairs that didn't exist before but which adds to the moral reasons for accepting Christ when it is appropriate to do so.

I also suggest that whether a person prays the prayer or not (and I do not insist on doing it in front of me or using this formula) that he or she must take seriously that God may have already provided for an answer somewhere already since one might expect that such a prayer would be possible for many people throughout history. Then I introduce some of the evidence for Christianity and invite them to look more deeply into the matter to see if this prayer was heard. I know one seeking person who was effectively led to Christ by praying this prayer, saying that this was just what she needed to hear.

Maybe you are in the same boat. You feel that you cannot responsibly receive the good that God would do you because you see no justification for God. Science seems to have the money in the bank that overrules any plausibility of theism. And yet it seems true to you that your whole being is meant for something rather than nothing. But it is possible to move from skepticism to faith through several gradual steps, each of which based on evidence is a rational risk. If you are willing to expectantly explore the case for God and for Christ you will find the way – because God will be guiding you – to a reasonable, healthy, mature adult and saving faith in Christ.

If this describes you or someone you care about, then I have prepared this little book for you as much as anyone else. It provides a summary of just the sort of evidence for Christianity mentioned here. You may want to pray the agnostic's prayer at the end of reading chapter 13.[1]

---

[1] Adapted from a post that appeared at "The Gnuvemberist" blog, July 2, 2012.

Table of Contents

Introduction: Notebook Apologetics

What is this book? First, let me make clear what it is not. It is not a scholarly work that offers original research nor does it claim to offer any fresh developments in any field. I do not claim to offer anything original or brilliant on the subject matter. I have used a sloppy footnote apparatus to connect the reader with works that are professional or creditable if the reader wants to go deeper into an issue and to credit where the original sources of the ideas here can be found.

Then what is this book? There is an old maxim that educational preparation is not meant to be hoarded but shared, especially seminary preparation. In my small local church, I helped entrepreneur a ministry to the adults of various ages who were getting excellent teaching in the form of regular Bible studies and sermons, but did not have more of an opportunity at church to learn about other important subjects and skills relevant to handling the Bible and living out the Biblical worldview. In particular, I wanted to help parents who were worried about the faith of their young adult children going out into the world and to college.

The group we formed took measures to be practical for busy adults. It was formed on the proposition that some Christians would be more receptive to challenging subjects if they explored such topics together with people from their own church community whom they trusted, rather than reading books on those topics or setting aside the time to take classes. Our small group met once every other week at someone's home. We would sit together in the living room and then after prayer, we would have an informal presentation with room for questions about the topic of the evening. After an hour, we would close with a prayer. We would relocate to the dining room for refreshments and an open-ended discussion of the subject for another half hour or so. Since I was responsible for this material, I would prepare the presentation for the evening. Then during the subsequent week I would write up the notes for the presentation, including discussions that came up because of it, and send them through the congregation's group email. This allowed those who could not make the meetings to still see the material and it allowed the meetings to be subject to the authority of the leadership. This also usually generated more feedback and discussion.

Over several years, we studied such things as Basic Biblical Practical Reasoning, Basic Biblical Interpretation, and Basic Christian Doctrine. After several years, we looked at Basic Christian Apologetics. Our experience confirmed that there is a great interest and demand for understanding defending the faith. The notes I published on email generated much attention and I was asked to make them more available. That is what this book is – Notebook Apologetics.

For this book, I wanted to preserve as much as possible the warm informal character of the learning environment. What I have done is clean up and polish the notes I distributed for this group, removing the personal discussions and adjusting it to a wider audience, as well as disciplining the liberties that come with an informal setting. I have added footnotes to indicate where I found the basic elements of these presentations so that others can know where to find them. I hope some of the flavor remains so that ordinary church members and young people will feel welcome in the book.

This book is an introduction and an invitation to apologetics, the discipline of defending the truth of the Christian faith. It is essentially a digest of material that I hope will be like salted peanuts to encourage Christians to dig deeper. I have presented the material to form a complete argument for the fundamental sources of Christian belief and thus a defense of the whole of the Christian faith. However, this book is no substitute for the reader taking the trouble to study these arguments and making them their own. An apologetic is more effective if it is your own work, a point I wish to teach by example here.

As Christians, God calls each of us to be prepared to give a defense for the reason for the hope that is within us to whomever asks. This defense must be proportioned to the ability, background, and maturity of the Christian.[2] Further, the need for an apologetic faith rather than an apologizing faith is especially vital in the world of the 21st century.

I want to thank Sue Thielke at Framework Productions and Martin Murphy at Theocentric Publishing Group for all of their generous help with the preparation of this book. I also want

---

[2] 1 Peter 3:15,16, English Standard Version, Crossway, 2006.
To listen to an audio exposition of this passage by the author, go to:
http://dl.dropbox.com/u/9929427/topicals/2005_04_03%20I%20Pet%203.1
5-16%20JH.mp3

to thank the Bible Application Seminar group without whom this book could not be: Douglas Weeks, Mark Weldon, Susan Woodruff, Dave Shetland, Andra Schadt, Nicole Schadt, and all the others who participated with us. I also want to thank Trinity Fellowship Church (CCCC) in Syracuse, New York for being my family in Christ all these years, especially the elders and deacons, and especially Jeremy Jackson for his irreplaceable oversight and friendship. I also thank all those who read and reviewed this manuscript for publishing: Douglas Weeks, Sue Woodruff, Sue Thielke, and Valerie Trautman. I also want to show appreciation for many friends and fellow travelers whose gifts, time, and feedback also contributed to the quality of this work: Dr. Jeremy Pierce, Matthew Saufley, Drs. Mark and Irem Kurtsal Steen, Bill and Nancy Finch, Paul J. Ryfun, and Raj Rao. Finally, I want to thank my late professor, good friend, and true mentor, Dr. W. Wynn Kenyon, a student of Dr. Jonathan Gerstner, for cultivating my interest in philosophy, apologetics, and theology in a godly and wholesome fashion, and to whom this book is dedicated.

None of these are responsible for anything that lacks in this book. That responsibility belongs only to me.

"Sing a song that sets you free.
Sing a song of Calvary.
I'm so happy! Yes, I am!
I've been washed in the Blood of the Lamb!"

Larry Norman

Part I

Meeting Objections to Faith

1. Plausibility Structures and Blank Stares

I. NEGATIVE AND POSITIVE APOLOGETICS

Many people struggle, lose their faith, or are prevented from faith because they are aware of some issue that they believe prevents them from believing in Christ with intellectual integrity. They experience a bad conscience over believing because they think that they have found something that makes some crucial Christian claim false. For example, many feel that they have experienced something that they would never expect a good God to allow happening to them in their lives. Since it did happen, they conclude that a good God does not exist. This becomes for them a defeater for believing in the Christian God.

This kind of concern illustrates the sort of reason someone could give for not coming to believe or ceasing to believe. An argument that tries either to prove a Christian claim to be false or which tries to prove that proposed support for a Christian claim fails is called a defeater for Christianity. What we are focusing on in Part I is how to deal with potential defeaters for Christian claims. Defeating defeaters is often called "negative apologetics". Apologetics is the discipline of defending one's faith The word "apologetics" comes from the Greek words apo ("back") and logos ("word"), and means "to give a word back", specifically to defend, as in a court of law. A famous example of this use of the word is in Plato's dialogue, the "Apology" where Socrates defends himself in court against the charges of corrupting Athenian youth. Negative apologetics is the practice of dealing with defeaters or objections against Christian faith. Positive apologetics, on the other hand, gives reasons for Christian faith. In Part I, we will focus on negative apologetics.

Positive apologetics is valuable for making as explicit as possible grounds for the reasonableness of Christian faith. It shows that believing is intellectually conscientious. This is a learned process that requires skill and work, but it is of great value to the church to know that such an enterprise is possible and that some are called to do it. However, it might seem to be clear that the foundations of Christian belief are already at least tacitly present in the minds of properly functioning and healthily developed people. For example, among the ideas for God one might have is the idea of an infinitely perfect being. Such an idea, though not, by definition, fully comprehensible, may be as apprehensible as the idea of infinity itself. It also may imply the necessity of its being actual. In this sense, the mind is intellectually attracted to God. Another factor is our sense of absolute dependence for being upon something other than ourselves. We are certain that we exist but also that we are not responsible for our existence and that we might not have existed. Such a sensibility draws us to look beyond ourselves to something sufficiently capable of bringing into and sustaining our being -- something which must ultimately depend on nothing else for its own being -- and thus we are led again to God.

Further, there is the sense of wonder at the gloriousness and awfulness we find when we consider our place in the total cosmos as well its orderly law-like nature, such as is described in

Psalm 8. It also seems clear that the idea of a God or an Ultimate God is widely dispersed throughout all human cultures and that even neurophysiological evidence tends to confirm a natural tendency to be religious. So it seems that religion is natural to humans apart from interference. There must be something that is preventing people from believing in God and thus being open to Christianity. Removing the obstacles to faith, although not enough to show that reason supports belief in God or Christianity, may have the immediate pastoral value of allowing a person's natural tendency to believe to proceed freely.

In experience it seems that unbelief has more to do with what blocks us from faith than with what pushes us to faith. Often that is very specific and different from individual to individual. We won't be able to address every possible concern but we will try to deal with several broad concerns that you can hopefully fine-tune to meet your specific needs.

II. ONE OF THE MOST PERNICIOUS ARGUMENTS AGAINST FAITH

Has something like this conversation ever happened to you?

Unbeliever: Why do you believe that the universe was created by God?

Believer: I believe that because the universe looks designed and because the Bible tells me so.

Unbeliever: (Silence, stares blankly, rolls eyes, has an "Oh, really?" expression on his face.)

Many Christians can think of times when this or something essentially like this happened to them. You may have heard your views being described as "quaint" or 'interesting" in the more polite versions of this. I will call these kind of conversation stopping responses to the expression of Christian views "Blank Stare Arguments". I once heard a distinguished philosopher critiqued tongue in cheek for not being sufficiently moved by blank stare arguments. Christians can expect to encounter many subtle blank stare arguments if they ever are called to express something that reveals their beliefs in our society.

Of course, and don't forget this, a "blank stare" argument is not really an argument. There is no reason given in a blank stare. A blank stare is a shaming device, a way of putting someone down. Blank stares send a message not only of intellectual failing but also moral or social failing to live up to one's cognitive duties or to be inadequately educated for one's class. It moves the person stared at from being in the OK status to the not-OK status. A blank stare is a form of offense giving, like calling someone a moron, because it regards the other as not even being worthy of a response. Now, as a form of offense giving, it can be legitimate or illegitimate. A person may truly have failed to meet intellectual obligations or failed to exhibit intellectual virtue or failed to maintain a responsible intellectual stewardship. We might greet someone who claimed that our society was being subliminally manipulated by a conspiracy of space aliens with an appropriate blank stare.

But a blank stare could be an illegitimate way of ending an awkward conversation by appealing to one's own credentials or presumed prestige. It can also be a way to enforce group boundaries as a form of social gate-keeping. The problem is that the legitimacy or illegitimacy of the response is often not clear to the victim. If the problem is that the person staring is aware of some specific piece of the latest evidence that another person would not know in the course of a busy life, then even if it is a defeater, the person is hardly guilty of not knowing it. If, however, the person should have learned, say, cross multiplication of fractions when they were taught it in grade school, the stare may be legitimate. The best thing is to confront the person staring, "Did I say something wrong? What's that look for?" However, psychologically, it can be very difficult to cope with shame and the person may just be shamed into silence or at least may think better of pursuing the matter under the circumstances, living to fight another day.

III. WORLDVIEWS AND PLAUSIBILITY STRUCTURES

But rather than being something in particular, a blank stare may indicate that one of the fundamental commitments of the person staring has been transgressed by the person being stared down, that the victim has strayed outside the staring persons plausibility structure. A plausibility structure is a set of core beliefs, often held as assumptions, which dictate for the person holding them what is and is not to be considered possible. If someone appeals to a claim which contradicts the other's set of core beliefs, then the person will regard it implausible, and hence may produce a blank stare. Even when a person is not in a position to respond to a blank stare, the recognition that a blank stare may be due to the other person's plausibility structure can help dismiss unnecessary shame a person might experience because of a blank stare. Our purpose in this chapter will be to provide help in analyzing the sources of plausibility structures to dispel the hint that the other must be giving you a blank stare because they know something you do not.

Fulfilling the role of a plausibility structure is one of the logical functions of a person's worldview. A worldview is a perspective of a person that is determined by a set of core beliefs, some of which can be made explicit in the form of propositions. The beliefs that make up a worldview are chosen because of the person's intent to believe only the truth and to make sense or understand the world and their life in it. It has theoretical and practical value. A worldview thus attempts to provide answers to questions like, What is ultimately real?, what is the nature of humanity?, what is the basis for my identity?, what is the origin and destiny of the world?, what things are most important in life, etc. Worldviews are personal but are also transmitted and shared and thus identify communities of people sharing an ultimate purpose. So we can define a worldview by determining a set of beliefs such that one must sincerely hold those beliefs to be considered a member in good standing of a community which aspires to live according to that worldview. This allows us to test a worldview. A worldview is true or justified if and only if its defining beliefs are true or justified.[3]

---

[3] See Harold A. Netland, *Dissonant Voices: Religious Pluralism and the Question of Truth*, (Regent College Publishing, 1999).

To reflect on one's worldview, to make it clear, to refine it, or correct it is a lifelong task that involves reflection and a desire for continuous learning. However, while everyone might be said to have a worldview, most have it not reflectively but tacitly. This is because such a view was only acquired by absorbing the assumptions of the practices one is taught in family, school, and culture. As one proverb has it, we rebel against the lessons our parents made a deliberate effort to teach us but simply assume the same things our parents assumed. Our assumptions remain until we deliberately question them. However, this does not just apply to children but also to adults. An important idea in education is the idea of a "hidden curriculum", that along side of the explicit aims and assignments of the curriculum, there is an implicit transmission of views and beliefs which taken up by the student because they are assumed by the curriculum formation process. This applies to higher education as well as elementary education. A person who has learned fundamentally different core beliefs may experience and intractable form of "culture shock" in a curriculum founded on contradictory core beliefs.

IV. THE MODERN WORLDVIEW:
THE HERETICAL IMPERATIVE

Charles Taylor[4] describes the history of western culture briefly in three periods:

---

[4] See Charles Taylor, *A Secular Age*, Belknap Press of Harvard University Press; 1st edition, 2007.

1. The Classical Medieval Period: Impossible not to believe in God -1500

2. The Early Modern Period: Possible to not believe in God - 1500 - 1850

3. The Contemporary Postmodern Period: Impossible to believe in God 1850 – now

The claim that it is now impossible to believe in God does not mean that no one today believes in God. It refers in part to the loss of God among those who are considered the wearers of the official robes of society, the authorities in the most established institutions which shape and direct the course of social development. In the present, that would be the professorates of the great universities and those who lead in government, media, and business. They have a great claim to be the most informed, most disciplined, and most objective executives of the knowledge industry, particularly in the sciences. This is an industry that has brought the greatest benefits of modern civilization - science, technology, medicine, national defense, administrative policy, and market efficiency. These are all enterprises that the public has come to greatly depend on and which most of the public is not able to understand. We thus have to allow the sovereignty of the professionals, including their presumption of authority. So if it is a matter of settled truth to that circle of intelligences that God could not exist, what can the average person really say except to either come forward and forgo their superstitions or hold to them quietly and privately. Here is the critical supernova of all blank stare arguments.

However, among the leaders of modern society there seems to be a commonly held worldview that functions as a gate keeper to restrict access to membership and which more or less hangs on three major core beliefs:

a. Scientific Naturalism - that the methods and assumptions of natural science are the only acceptable conditions for adopting beliefs as true. Unless you can proportion your belief to the evidence, which must be measurable empirical evidence, your belief is not justified. Thus the only things that can be said to exist are material 'objects' physically interacting with each other, matter in motion. Anything else must be an illusion.

b. Metaphysical Nihilism - Except in the sense that nature can be described as extended masses whose behavior can be described as regular, there is no other sense in which nature is intelligible because there is no other feature to the real world that is a possible object of reasoning. Hence there are no essences, persons, purposes, perfections, or prescriptions intrinsic to nature and hence no way in which nature makes sense. Only brute states of affairs exist.

c. Creative Relativism - Because of Metaphysical Nihilism there is no basis for morality or meaning in life. Moral and cultural points of view are just an aspect of cultural evolution and there is no ground for evaluation for one's own culture or another's. Nor is there any reason to sacrifice the enjoyment of these momentary pleasures and little wonders in our day to day life for pursuing a greater truth. To insist otherwise is a form of bigotry at best or empty sacrifice at worst. Thus tolerance is the only possible virtue if anything is virtuous. But there is nothing that stands in the way of the person who creates new points of view and new values and new rights, ad infinitum, as nothing else but the assertion and actualization of his own will.

Lesslie Newbigin, following Peter Berger, calls this view the "Heretical Imperative"[5], the view that just because you can, you must come up with views that radically deviate from conventions as much as possible, that each individual at each separate moment must strive to develop a new "heresy". The only thing that is sacred and not to be heretically abandoned is science.

We wouldn't want to assert that every influential and and/or superiorly trained professor holds this view. Many evangelicals and other dissenters have been successful in the academy and become respected experts in these fields.[6] But many have observed that this seems to be the dominant research plausibility structure in the highest ranking institutions in the west. This worldview determines which possibilities will be accepted as worthwhile projects as well as which intellectuals will be received.

---

[5] See Lesslie Newbigin, *Foolishness to the Greeks: The Gospel and Western Culture*, William B. Eerdmans Publishing Company, 1986.

[6] D. Michael Lindsay, *Faith in the Halls of Power: How Evangelicals Joined the American Elite*, Oxford University Press, 2007.

I am suggesting that a worldview that is held by the great opinion leaders will become the dominant plausibility structure for the general society just through passive assimilation. This is clearly too simple of a picture to explain everything but it may account for much. The question is whether it must be true that the opinion leadership necessarily holds this worldview based on reason or whether it is possible that social factors not related to reason determine their views. If the latter, then society's general and tacit acceptance of this view, expressed by blank stares, will not be a sufficient reason to discredit the beliefs of Christians.

V. WORLDVIEWS AND INSTITUTIONAL ANALYSIS

In this section I will briefly explain several accounts by social scientists, that give some explanatory plausibility that views held and transmitted by respected institutions may be due to social factors rather than superior evidence. As a group I will call this Institutional Analyses. Institutional Analysis is the study of institutions that discovers whether or not the assertions made by professionals are determined by social factors rather than the force of the evidence.

A. Robert Wuthnow and Threatened Disciplines: Wuthnow is a sociologist who has published on religion, science, and secularization. In his work he has discovered that there are a significantly greater proportion of agnostics/atheists than religious believers in academic institutions. But he points out this percentage reveals something different when analyzed by university department. In the natural sciences department, there is standardly no significant difference between the number of theists and the number of atheists/agnostics among research scientists. Being in the natural sciences in an institution of higher learning is no predictor of atheistic belief. However, as we move into the social sciences, things change. In psychology, sociology, and economics there is a significantly higher percentage of atheists to theists, and in the humanities the percentage is higher still. Wuthnow concludes that there is a correlation between the increasing percentage of atheists/agnostics to theists as you go from the natural sciences to the social sciences to the humanities, and the degree to which the discipline members are insecure about their persistence as an academic discipline.

This perception seems to be based on whether the discipline can justify its existence by the standard of the methods of natural science. Since the natural sciences are the paradigm they perceive no threat to their discipline. On the other hand, there are dissimilarities between the methods of social sciences and natural sciences. Social science relies on qualitative research, participant observation, oral interpretation, naturally occurring settings (rather than controlled experiments) and so on to such a point where some natural scientists simply deny that social sciences are science at all. Thus the perception that unless social scientists can establish their credentials against science, they will not be considered as really adding to the body of knowledge and thus they could lose their place in the university. Even more threatened are the humanities, which originally were not perceived to be doing any kind of research at all in any scientific sense. Now the humanities generate courses on psychoanalytic theory, Marxian social theory, gender theory, colonial and post colonial theory, in order to get some "theory" and create the impression that some kind of informative research is taking place. The evidence seems to suggest that discouraging the production of theistic scholars is a way to preserve credibility with the institution and to preserve the discipline. So in the departments that have little to fear from being compared to natural science, there is no indication that either theism or atheism is favored.[7]

B. Thomas Kuhn and Dominant Research Paradigms: Probably the most well known account of social factors in knowledge production was applied to the history of natural science itself by Thomas Kuhn. Prior to Kuhn, the philosophy of science tried to argue that all thought ought to be modeled on the method of science or be considered meaningless. It also held that the method of science was empirical verification of hypotheses. If a hypothesis did not have verification conditions that were fulfilled by experiment and the force of evidence they were meaningless. Kuhn observed the work of real scientists throughout the records of the history of science and discovered that scientists did not necessarily follow the approach described by the philosophers. In fact, he argued that what determines which theories were pursued and which left behind was determined by factors that had nothing to do with the force of evidence. In his book, The Structure of

---

[7] See Robert Wuthnow, "Science and the Sacred", in *The Sacred in a Secular Age: Toward Revision in the Scientific Study of Religion*, ed. Phillip E. Hammond, University of California Press, 1985.

Scientific Revolutions, he argued that what was seen to be of scientific value was shaped by rival paradigms.

The classic case was the situation in the early modern period when there was a rivalry between the older Scholastic commitment to Aristotelian Universal 'biology' which explained by appeal to natural ends, and "Corpuscularianism" which explained things by appeal to just atomic particles and motion. According to Kuhn, there was no fact that showed that one was true and the other false or that one was better than the other, but there were several social and political conditions that were associated with each view which created a struggle that eventually swept up Galileo. According to Kuhn, scientists determine what counts as evidence by the assumption made by the theory they prefer which creates a case of circular reasoning. The defenders of a particular theory actually resist possible counterevidence to give the theory a chance to prove itself over time rather than claiming the counter evidence refutes the theory. Often the choice of different proposals depends on how well it fits with particular institutions. Once the choice is made and the view becomes the dominant view, it resists for various reasons other than evidence (named researchers, financial, political) alternative evidence and theories, until social factors allow for another revolution. We need not accept the extreme version of Kuhn's view at the time he wrote this book that all science was only determined by social factors, but some science is. Kuhn did document various ways that even natural science is socially influenced, and showed the scientists were not governed by a single ideal way of evaluating evidence.

C. Frederich Hayek and Cultural Evolution: Hayek was an economist and social scientist who had a conversion regarding the role cultural selection played in forming traditions. At first, his approach to social science was to be guided by the same methods as the natural sciences, but he discovered that ordinary people prospered more following their traditional institutional beliefs while social scientists and economists theories often proved to be counterproductive. He began to suspect that tradition was a more reliable guide than science when it came to fulfilling the healthy interests of people. He observed that the things that played an important role in the success of average people had to do with following their entrenched moral and religious beliefs. However, moral and religious beliefs could only be considered meaningless by science. But he came to think that science itself was hampered by its inability to test theories and practices over the long term. Long term practice testing is actually accomplished by a traditional commitment to the practice and the ability of the community to flourish over the long haul rather than perish. In this sense, a process like evolution picked the societies whose traditions allowed them to flourish, and so the burden of proof is on breaking with tradition. Hayek's account is interesting because it indicates that the scientific experts, precisely because such experts are driven by their gifted talents and their commitment to scientism, became systematically mistaken about their policy claims. We tend to think that if you are smart and informed you are not likely be wrong, but it could be that it is in being smart and informed in the defined sense of science that contributes to one's not being right.

So Wuthnow, Kuhn, and Hayek, provide illustrations as to how great expertise may be compatible with great error.

VI. CONCLUSION AND CAUTION

We looked at the problem of blank stares from individuals and also especially the collective blank stare of high culture. We looked at one source of blank stares in the plausibility structure that comes with the particular worldviews. We also argued that worldview formation is often tacit rather than explicit (and recommended the conscious life long process of continuous worldview formation). We also argued that worldview formation could be tacit in adults as well as children. And we argued that there are several ways in which a worldview can become the dominant and controlling worldview even among research professionals in ways other than following the evidence wherever it leads.

So we conclude that, at best, the average person on the street who gives us a blank stare is simply echoing what top leaders of opinion are taking as their fundamental view of the world. However, some institutional analysis gives us reason not to necessarily accept these views of the authorities because it may be that they are determined by vested purposes rather than the force of the evidence even in greatly skilled minds. As Socrates observes in the Euthyphro, when the gods go to war they don't do it over questions about measuring, but rather over what should be regarded as important. When it comes to intellectuals, they come in both theist and atheist types. If the gods disagree, why should we expect more from smart humans? So in the last analysis, anyone who gives a blank stare – including the Christian believer – had better be prepared to give a reason for their view.

However, we should distinguish between institutional analysis in the strong sense and institutional analysis in the weak sense. In the weak sense, institutional analysis shows us that it is not necessarily the case that the experts are justified. But in the strong sense, institutional analysis is said to show us that it is necessarily not the case that the experts are justified. We affirm institutional analysis in the weak sense but deny it in the strong sense. If the strong sense were right, no one could be justified in anything they believed, including the strong version of institutional analysis. We would certainly all be in the same boat but it would have already sunk. All we have done is given grounds that make it rational not to be intimidated by blank stares but we have not removed the need to provide a defense of the faith by responding to objections.

2. The Problem of Evil

When we discuss evil and suffering, we need to make a distinction in general between problems and mysteries. That is, we need to distinguish between what is tractable and what is intractable. Problems are tractable. We can fully understand them and discover an adequate solution to them. They are situations which are intelligible in themselves and also to us. A mystery is intractable. It is something that surpasses our ability to understand because of our limits, and yet is still something that is not brute or unexplained. A mystery is intelligible in itself but not to us. It is something that God understands but not us. Problems have solutions. Mysteries do not, but they do have clues. When we think about a problem, then perhaps we eventually after several generations see through it and solve it. But with mysteries, we may contemplate it forever but only understand it asymptotically but never completely. We deal with problems with action. We deal with mysteries with contemplation.

Referring to our discussion in the previous chapter, the modern day plausibility structure tends to have no room for mysteries. The working assumption is that situations are either problems that will be solved eventually or they are not problems because there is no solution - that is they are just brute situations. This claim fits the view that the only tools in the box are those of science and technology. If all you have is a hammer, the whole world is either a nail or it is nothing at all. However, the Christian believes in a God high and lifted up, the infinite eternal and holy Being, Creator of all. God himself is a mystery to us, a being we can apprehend but not comprehend. As the great doctors of the church have said, God is Darkness to us not because He is not light but because He is Light Inapproachable. It is therefore possible that there are many things about life that are true and only proportional to his infinite understanding and not ours, namely mysteries. In a theistic universe, mysteries are not surprising.

It is possible then and we think that it is true that suffering is a mystery that we can only have an approximate understanding about. Of course, the great painfulness of suffering may tend to make us want to demand an exhaustive account of things (and right now) but it may be that we can only get closer and closer to understanding suffering. In this light, we find all kinds of clues in the Scriptures about the various uses of suffering in the life of the believer as well as the non-believer, and indeed of the whole universe. These along with the raw experience of suffering provide a rich picture which may not fully answer our questions but neither will it undermine legitimate hopes.

I want to do two things. In this chapter, I want to deal with those who think that evil is a problem for believers, and that it shows that belief in God must be false. In the next chapter, I want to say a very little bit about the mystery of suffering. The first deals with the intellectual problem of evil and the second with the experiential mystery of suffering.

II. WHAT IT MEANS TO SAY THERE IS EVIL IN THE WORLD

Consider comparing a goat with a human being that has suffered severe brain damage. It is true of both that they do not have the capacity to think. It is also true that having the capacity to think is a capacity that is great to have. But we do not think that the lack of the capacity to think makes a goat a bad goat. It is natural that a goat does not think. However, we say that the lack of thinking in the brain damaged human is bad. A human is supposed to be able to think. This is what makes not being able to think bad for a human but not a goat. This suggests that badness or evil is not anything in itself, but rather the absence of something that should be present. The Medievals, especially Augustine, captured this by defining evil as not a thing but a privation of a previously existing perfection.[8]

A good example is the concept of illness. When we say that someone is ill, we do not say that someone has something that a healthy person does not have, but rather that an ill person lacks something that a healthy person is supposed to have, namely the proper functioning of their body. Similarly "evil", like the word "lack", is a term used to refer to an absence rather than a presence. Strictly speaking then, evil is not anything in itself. Sin, as a mode of evil, is a lack of rectitude in our desires, intentions, or conduct. Sin is a want of conformity to the image of God's character in the human soul.

---

[8] St. Augustine, *The City of God*, Book XII, Chapters 1 – 9.

Therefore, it is not necessary for evil to exist for good to exist. However, it is necessary for good to exist in order for evil to be possible, since there must be some pre-existing good in order for any good to go missing. "Evil" then refers not to anything in itself but to a kind of state of affairs. Even a devil is just an angel that has fallen.

Another point we want to make about evil is that it begs the question to identify evil merely with suffering. The modern worldview that denies anything that cannot be measured by science and which is nihilistic about any moral absolutes tends to view evil as merely pain. However, if God and the soul exist, there may be many kinds of evil, in particular injustice and sin. Further, evil without anyone suffering and suffering without any evil is possible. Since the good lies in the presence of the proper functioning of something, one can imagine a case where a person's soul is properly functioning but not the body, while you could have another case where the body is fine but the soul is not. So you can have a righteous soul in a sick body or a healthy body with an unrighteous soul.

What this means is that there is a sense which we can say that "evil does not exist". What we mean by "evil" does not entail that there must be a rival cause other than God for all the evil in the world. However, this still is not enough to deal with the problem of evil as many see it. The question for them is, granting that evil is a kind of state of affairs, then how could or why would a good God allow it?

III. EVIL AS A PROBLEM FOR GOD

If you ask an atheist why they don't believe in God, one of the most common reasons they give is that the world is too evil for there to be a God. We certainly can see how one might feel that that is true but what are the actual merits of this response as an argument? The atheist's argument is this:

"If there was God, then there wouldn't be any evil in the world, but obviously there is some evil in the world, so God doesn't exist."

Here the idea is that the mere fact of evil is enough to prove that God does not exist. The Christian, even given the claim that evil is not anything in itself, doesn't want to deny the truth that there is evil in the world, understood as a state of affairs. One also would not want to deny the validity of the reasoning being used, which is a straightforward deduction. So to challenge the conclusion, we have to look closely at the support for the claim that if God exists, then evil would not. Why think that? Well, that also seems to be a straightforward deduction. Says the atheist:

"According to Christians, God is both omnipotent and be-nevolent. But an omnipotent being necessarily could remove all evil. And a benevolent being necessarily would remove all evil. So if God exists, there would be no evil since he could and would remove it necessarily."

Here the atheist is assuming that God is all powerful and all good for the sake of argument. The strength of what he says comes from the reasonable view that Christians would not deny that God is omnipotent or benevolent. We certainly would not deny that God is like that (although we would say that God's omnipotence is limited to doing only what is logically possible. He cannot make a square circle but this is one of the perfections of God rather than an imperfection). We also would not question the logic of the argument either. However, the argument only succeeds if both of those premises concerning omnipotence and benevolence which state what must necessarily be the case are really what must necessarily be the case. If either one is false, then the argument is not sound. I will focus solely on one of the claims: Is it really necessarily true that a benevolent being would remove all evil? Could it be that a benevolent being would allow the existence of some evil?

But before we can discuss that, we have to remember that there are different kinds of evil and that depending on the type of evil, one response may not work as well for one type as another. If there is a type of evil that a benevolent being necessarily would remove but which exists then the atheist's argument is successful. One kind of evil is when persons act immorally. So is it true that a benevolent God would remove all immoral conduct?

Notice that it is not necessary to have a matter of fact answer to this question. All we need is a plausible and consistent answer to refute a claim that something is necessarily true as a matter of conceivability. The atheist is arguing that a benevolent God would not allow evil because he cannot conceive of a possibility where such a God would. If something is necessarily true then it is true in all possible cases. But if there is a possible case where it is not true, then it is not necessarily true. To show something is possible all we need is a consistent story where God is benevolent but allows immorality. Any story that fits these requirements is traditionally called a "theodicy", a justification of God.

So is there a theodicy for the problem of immorality? Imagine two worlds or rather two ways God might have created the world. One way would be to make it such that everybody with a will necessarily does what is morally good all the time because they cannot do otherwise. The other way is to make a world where everyone is free to choose to be good or not. Which world is better? One could argue that in fact the second is better than the first because if people are good all the time because they cannot not be, then there is no real merit to their goodness. No one compliments gravity itself for keeping us on the planet because it could not do otherwise. In a world where it was up to people to be good by their own choice, then they do merit by doing good. So a world where people may merit by doing the moral good when they could have done evil is better than a world where people do good "automatically", even though such a world involves the real possibility that people will choose the bad rather than the good. So it is not necessarily the case that a good God would prevent all immorality.

Again, suppose that there are two other ways the world might go. In one way, people automatically start by being good and stay good through their lives because it is so easy to be good in that world. In another way, the world is such that no one is automatically good but must work to become good by facing temptation, suffering, doubt, struggle, and loneliness, and consistently having to choose to do the right thing, thus becoming virtuous through effort. It seems that God would prefer the second way to the first because there is no real merit to the consistent good behavior of the people of the first way the world might go while the people of the second world are worthy of their accolades. But to make that world would be to make a world in which there is great suffering and evil treatment from others. So again, it is not necessarily the case that a good God would prevent all immorality.

The insight we get from cases like these is that our intuitions about moral goodness involve authentic responsibility and virtue, which involves meaningful choice and exposure to vulnerability. This means allowing for the possibility of moral failure. However, a world where we find genuine moral responsibility and merit is significantly more worthwhile than the lack of them.

But there is another kind of evil, the evil we see done in nature, that does not seem to be addressed by these theodicies, namely the evil that happens in the world but which is not the direct responsibility of human agency, such as tsunamis, earthquakes, forest fires, and so on. Wouldn't a good God remove all natural evil if not all moral evil? "But natural evil exists, so God does not exist." Again let us look at two ways the world might have been. In one way, the natural world behaves irregularly and unpredictably. It is constantly in every place being tweaked, suspended, twisted, shifted, and again and again so that nothing can be expected to happen based on what already happened. On the other hand, another way the world might behave is consistent, according to natural regularities or natural laws, so that it is possible to make predictions of the behavior of the world and control for it. Which would you rather live in? It seems the second one because the regularity of natural laws makes planning and foresight possible. In an unpredictable world, there would be no point in preparing for the future since there is no way of meaningfully anticipating or managing for the future. Such planning is important for the development of character. But a world that operated according to the laws of nature will also have earthquakes and tidal waves and so on. So it is better to live in a world with certain naturally destructive phenomena than a world that is arbitrary. So it is not necessarily the case that a good God would prevent all natural evil.

IV. EVIL AND THE SOVEREIGNTY OF GOD

And so a crucial premise of the atheist's argument is false. It is not necessarily true that a benevolent God would remove all evil, whether we are talking about immorality or natural evil.

But the atheist will continue by saying, "Isn't it true that the Christian view of God not only has it that He is omnipotent and benevolent, but also sovereign?" The Bible pictures God as being in control of all affairs, such as the hardening of Pharaoh's heart and foreseeing the betrayal of Judas. If God sees to whatever comes to pass, how is humanity free in the sense of meaningful freedom illustrated by these theodicy stories? The answer is that with respect to human choice and agency, virtue is still fragile per se and contingent upon a human being's ability to see what is good and right, the accumulation of his or her character from his or her previous behavior through habit forming, and the circumstances regarding the degree of temptation in each opportunity of making a choice a person faces.

God is able, being presumed to be omnipotent, to determine the circumstances and see to it that history proceeds according to His own plan without overriding the genuine agency and responsibility of human beings. Their actions have genuine merit or demerit, although made certain to occur. Although given God's plan there will be no alternative history to the one that occurs in our world, this does not take away responsibility from humans as one might expect. Suppose you have a prisoner who is just as content to stay in his cell when the door is unlocked as when it is locked. Then he is as freely staying in his cell in one case as the other. Similarly, humans are able to act freely even though no other history is allowed to happen under God's control. Finally, this does not necessarily make God the author of evil because while the motives people have for doing an act may be evil, God's motives for allowing humans to act according to their evil motives may be good. "You meant it for evil, but God meant it for good".

But then the atheist will argue quite reasonably, "If all that were true, then that would mean that you could still have free will, responsibility, and virtue while under God's control. But that would undermine your rebuttal to my argument because it means that God could have created a world free of moral evil without denying human freedom or merit, and so if he were benevolent He necessarily would have. Furthermore, isn't it true that, according to the Christian message, in heaven all people will be good all the time? Is it not the case that in the Garden of Eden, mankind was protected from all kinds of natural evil by the intervention of God? How can Christians consistently claim that a world of freedom and natural laws is really better as the theodicies argue?" They can because the case of Heaven and Eden are not to be understood as standalone scenarios but rather as a part of a complete story that has God dealing with man's sin at the heart of it. Eden was held in its integrity as a place of probation for Adam where he could remain in long as he obeyed God. God's testing of Adam was genuine. It was by Adam's own hand that corruption came to the rest of the human race.

But God provided the solution by giving his only Son to be a substitute for us. Even though he was God of God and thus morally perfect, the merit by which he would be able to substitute himself for our sins had to be an accomplished merit through the facing of struggle and temptation. That is, he had to acquire virtue at the point where Adam failed to do so. Christians are saved by accepting Christ's merit for their sins but this is a real choice they make to repent and believe and to live a life of trust and obedience. By faith alone they eventually receive heaven but this gift is not isolated from their having trusted in Christ. It is because of this that they are able to live consistently as good people in heaven. So the status of mankind in these various states -Eden, the Fall, redemption, and glory - are all necessarily connected with human responsibility for sin and Christ's merit. In other words, these special events form the logic of a larger history such that while the existence of humanity existing sinless is hypothetically possible and good, there is an even greater good that will be realized in God's plan, but only if God provides for some evil. As far as we can tell, it may be that no good greater than the good of just a sinless humanity is logically possible without such a provision for evil. However, since we accepted that not being able to do the logically impossible is not an imperfection of God's power, we have not run afoul of the other premise in the atheist's argument from evil. God could be both all-powerful and benevolent in bringing about a history that has some evil but which thus brings about an even greater good.

With this way of thinking about the matter, we can understand why the Christian presents the cross as the ultimate theodicy. On the cross, God in Jesus Christ receives the retribution for all sin freely on behalf of all history, and this was already intended as part of God's plan before creation.[9]

V. IS THERE MORE EVIL THAN A GOOD GOD WOULD ALLOW?

The atheist, though, is not finished. Granted that it may not necessarily be the case that a benevolent God would not remove all evil, isn't it true that so much of the evil in the world and even the total amount of evil in the world has no reason for it? Take Dostoevsky's story in The Brothers Karamazov about the landowner who has a small child mauled to death in front of his own mother for laming his hound accidentally with a stone. The boy cannot be accused of being responsible for that, nor

---

[9] See John S. Feinberg, *The Many Faces of Evil*, Crossway; Rev Exp edition, 2004 for more on evil and the Sovereignty of God.

could getting mauled contribute to the boy's virtue, nor was it the result of natural laws. There seems to be no apparent justification for it, and that is probably because there is no justification for it. The atheist argues:

"Okay, so if God is good there would be no unjustified evil. But it is reasonable to believe that there is some unjustified evil. So God does not exist."

Here "unjustified evil" means evil that cannot be accounted for by free will or character building or natural laws or anything else. It is evil for which there is no good reason. So in this case, unlike the first argument, the Christian will agree that if God exists then there could not be any evil without good reason. "You meant it for evil, but God meant it for good." must apply for any evil one discovers in the world in some legitimate way or another. So the Christian is willing to accept that there is evil, but is not going to accept that there is any unjustified evil. What is the argument for the existence of unjustified evil? The atheist replies:

"I can't demonstrate that there is unjustified evil but I can show that no reasonable person can deny that there is unjustified evil. There is evil like the mauled boy that we do not see any explanation for. It could be that the reason we see no explanation is that there really is no explanation for it. Not only that, but that seems to be the most plausible explanation for it, because it is the simplest. So a reasonable person must think that there is no explanation for it and that it is unjustified evil. So you have to accept that there is unjustified evil in the world, since cases like the mauled boy can be found everywhere."

Here is an example of a legitimate attempt to infer from the evidence to the best explanation for it, a common rational procedure. In this argument, the evidence compels but does not prove the conclusion. It could still be true given the evidence that the conclusion is false. But we cannot simply ignore a compelling case, as long as all three conditions listed in the atheist's argument are met. In this case, a Christian will agree that there seems to be no explanation to cases like the mauled boy and also that one possible explanation is that there is no answer to why the boy was allowed to be mauled. So that leaves the claim that this is the best explanation left to be challenged. Is it?

Often we think that it is. I think that there are no such things as ghosts or UFOs because I have never seen one. This is because nothing in my background leads me to expect them. However, in this case the background has already been provided for us by the atheist. The atheist started us off by assuming that God is omnipotent and benevolent. The question really is, assuming that such a God exists, is the most reasonable explanation for these cases that there is no explanation? The Christian can confidently say "no". An alternative explanation for why we can't see an explanation is that the matter is too deep for us but not for God, that it is a "mystery". God is in a position far better than us to know what is good to include in the world and what is not, and He may have reasons which we cannot fathom. So there could be a reason that God can see but we can't. And given that the God we are talking about is the God who is all powerful and benevolent, this is the most likely reason. At least, it is far from clear that there isn't a better reason than that there simply is no explanation. So the atheist's conclusion remains moot.

The atheist may try to get out of the case by saying that he only allowed that God was all powerful and all good and nothing else. And such a God is not enough to avoid making the "no explanation" explanation the most reasonable. But if atheists say that, that nullifies the whole project since the Christian was willing to accept that God was all powerful and all good, not that God was not anything else but all powerful and all good. That is not the Christian God. The Christian God is the infinitely perfect being of which being all powerful and all good is only a partial description. If that was the original target, it is not clear that being a mystery is not a better explanation than no explanation. The atheist has not met the burden of evidence that he has assumed from the beginning.[10]

Of course, if we ask which is the best explanation for the evidence, we have much other evidence to consider besides that we don't see a justification for many evil acts. Added to that is also the evidence for design in our DNA and the cosmological science that suggests that the universe had a beginning and thus a Beginner. There is also the evidence of our conscience of objective right and guilt. We will examine some of this evidence in our second part of this book. We should, both atheist and theist, ask what the better explanation is for all of this taken together.

---

[10]For more on the problem of evil, see Daniel Howard-Snyder, "God, Evil, and Suffering", from *Reason for the Hope Within*, Michael Murray ed., Wm. B. Eerdmans Publishing Company, 1998.

And then there is evil itself. What are we to make of evils like the Holocaust and human trafficking? It seems that it is inadequate to say that such evils are mere cases of human suffering. Our intuition is that they are evil in a much stronger sense. But our judgment that such cases are truly evil, does not make the best sense against a background that says everything came about from nothing but matter and chance.

VI. FROM THE PROBLEM TO THE MYSTERY

I hope this chapter shows that there is much to be said against the attempt to refute theism by appeal to evil.

But while there are good reasons the theist may give against the argument from evil, there remains a huge gulf between dealing with the intellectual problems of evil and encountering real suffering and evil in our lives. In the first case, we can address intellectual problems with argument but the question in the encounter with suffering is not how can we see the solution to the puzzle of suffering but how can we cope with the suffering that remains mysterious to us even while it remains so terribly painful and apparently arbitrary. This cannot be dealt with by argument but only with genuine pastoral care. We have only partially spoken to that by our distinction between mysteries and problems, by saying that suffering is a mystery rather than a problem, one for which the Bible has given us many clues. Furthermore, from the atheistic alternative there seems to be no meaning to suffering nor any fellowship in suffering nor is there any point for a love willing to suffer, either for us or by us, but on the Christian view there is always a meaning to suffering and to be realized in suffering, even if we don't fully understand and that in fact for these sufferings Christ has already suffered in our behalf. I have more to say about this in the next chapter.

3. Dealing with Suffering in Christ

In our last chapter, we looked at some of the intellectual and evidential issues regarding the problem of evil and offered the main lines of a response to the arguments against God from evil. Here we will deal with the experiential problem of suffering. As we said, dealing with the intellectual problems of evil is inadequate for coping with what can and does actually happen to Christians. The book of Job is eloquent testimony of this, but so also are the many real life tragedies faced by human beings, including believers. Many find ready solace in the various counsels and promises in the Scriptures. But in some cases, the believer feels almost washed away by perplexity and sorrow. It's on these cases where we hope to say something worthwhile. Our aim though is not to deal with objections to belief as before, but to provide an outline for direction for those who suffer and those who minister to them. Here I am addressing not a specialized class of ministers but every member of the church. I also address those who don't believe to paint a picture of the resources within belief for dealing with suffering.

However, this also has an important purpose in our defense of the faith. Christianity is argued to be true and to resist objections. But it also claims to be more than just the truth but also to speak it in love. Love, however, is much more vague and concrete. Here I hope to offer at least a substantive gesture in addressing the pain that is often behind the objections given in the previous chapter. A small hopeful gesture is much better than being left in the dark.

As we begin, I must confess my own sense of inadequacy about this. I don't see myself as being as gifted in this as other Christians or pastors. What I offer here is not original with me and my relation to this stuff is the same as those I am trying to reach out to. But we cannot avoid these issues and we must in due time seek answers. So I hope that this will serve as a beginning point rather than a complete answer.

II. THRIVING IN THE MIDST OF THE HOLOCAUST

Dr. Viktor Frankl was working on a new approach to psychology when the Nazis imprisoned him for being a Jew. While in a concentration camp, he noticed specific differences in those who endured and those who broke down. Those who endured and who were able reach out and minister to others rather than not were those who had a reason to live, who felt that there was a purpose to their lives that required their survival. This was Frankl's case as well; he sensed a need to publish his work, the manuscript that he kept hidden from the Nazis until the Allies came. In fact, the point of this work was that man's fundamental need was a meaning to life. As long was this was perceived to be satisfiable, a person could endure any trial.[11]

The source of meaning for Christians is their union with Christ through their faith and the promise of the indwelling Holy

---

[11] Viktor E. Frankl, *Man's Search for Meaning*, Pocket Books; Revised Updated edition, 1997.

Spirit. The cultivation of the believer's connection with Christ by faith is what enables him to make sense of most of his suffering. However, sometimes something happens that is so traumatic and perplexing, that the believer's faith is significantly shaken. While his bond with Christ cannot be broken, his own sense of that bond has become lost. He loses his assurance that Christ is worthy of his trust. Thus, his plight has come between himself and God. So the aim of direction in such suffering is twofold; first to encourage the afflicted believer to recover the sense that what God has done in his or her life has a purpose, even if he or she does not see what that purpose is, and second to encourage the believer to choose to surrender to that purpose in order to once again by in the center of God's will for him or her. In short, the aim is to help the believer reconnect with Christ. Since what is required is a way of seeing, this requires so much more than words. We must live with the believer in such a way that he or she may find a place to stand which has a vista for seeing Christ. We must be like Christ so that they might see Christ.

III. "LOOK WHAT GOD HAS DONE TO ME!"

What distinguishes ordinary suffering from these serious cases is that in the serious case we are sorely tempted to be angry with God. Anger is an emotion that is equal parts a feeling of moral disapprobation and the instinct of self-preservation. We feel that something is happening to us that is unjust and also threatening to us and ours. This accounts for the intensity of feeling in anger and its ability to bring about changes in the static parts of our lives. Anger involves both intense feeling but also judgment. The righteousness of our anger is according to the quality of our judgment, which may be rash or astute. One way to deal with anger is to examine the judgment that it presupposes.

When we feel anger at God, it's often because something has happened that we didn't really expect God to allow. At the time we might have felt that we were in God's will and expected to flourish in God's way, and then something comes up that seems to sabotage those expectations. We feel perplexed and do not know how to go further. At times like this, we appreciate the example set by Job and the Psalms. Rather than tolerating simplistic answers, the saints are bold to make their complaints about God to God and before God. They set the example that God does not want us to hide our thoughts and feelings from Him, but to tell Him everything.

In prayer, whether in mute silence or out loud with tears, we bring out and commit ourselves to what we see to be the case, but in God's presence with the expectation that God will hear us and can and may act on what we say. Praying then is not the same thing as grumbling and doing nothing. Compare prayer to a case where an employee has a legitimate complaint against his boss. If the company the employee works for does not have a grievance procedure which allows complaints to be passed on to upper management to deal with the employee's superiors, the employee is forced with the decision to either live with the injustice or take the matter up with an outside agency like the media. But if such a procedure for hearing complaints is available, it shows that the company intends to make a good faith effort to deal with problems from its bosses. In that case, the employee would be wrong to go outside the company before giving it a chance to deal with the problem itself. In a similar way, God in the Scriptures encourages his people to come to Him frankly with their complaints and perplexities. It is all right to tell God how He seems to make you feel. However, not every kind of complaining is desirable, not the Pharisees complaints about Jesus behind his back, for example. When we complain to God rightly, we do so with the hope that God hears and acts. As Job said, "Though he slay me, yet will I trust Him." We have the choice to turn to God with our anger or to turn away from God in our anger, but the burden of proof lies on doing the second. It may not be exactly clear what would satisfy the burden of proof here but hypothetically it may be the sort of thing that you know when you see it.

IV. GROWTH AND SIDETRACKING

However, God is free in how He might answer such a prayer and circumstances may actually give the suffering believer the opportunity to wait and to learn to patiently cope with the perplexity. It is often the case that people do not really begin searching for answers until they are deeply perplexed, until many of the gratuitous assumptions have been shot down. If they were in the position to see this happening to someone else, they might say that in spite of their perplexity, they are better off than they were before because they have been separated from their trite opinions and are now seeking for the truth. But when it is you, it is hard to see that this may be the case.[12]

People in pain will try to negotiate their way through it by "making deals with reality" trying to cut their losses.[13] Often this may include finding a substitute goal for their original goal which winds up compromising their own real interests. In the case of the believer, this may involve departing from the believer's calling by adopting a pseudo-calling that may preoccupy them for years without ultimately satisfying them. They need to be encouraged to return and face the issue that led to their separation from their purpose before they are tempted to despair of God's working in their life. The temptation is to avoid perplexity and suffering, but doing so also avoids the work that God may be accomplishing through suffering. God may be doing a deeper work of soul-making, being dissatisfied with the progress being made. This discipline facilitates the believer's sense of the meaning of suffering because it affects her dispositions and brings her to a place where she can see again. Christians must choose to accept and cooperate with rather than resist God's work.

V. LIFE IN THE BODY OF CHRIST

Paul tells us to bear one another's burdens because we all have our own burden to carry. It is plain as the sun to the suffering person that no one is experiencing exactly what they are

---

[12] Cp. Meno in Plato's dialogue *The Meno.*
[13] See Elisabeth Kubler-Ross, *On Death and Dying*, Scribner; 1st Edition, 1997.

experiencing, so to hear things like, "I know how you feel" will ring absolutely hallow.

Christians cannot assume to be able to experience another person's suffering for them. But we can help bear another's burdens by feeling with them rather than for them. In this the individual is helped when it's true that if one suffers, the whole body suffers. In this, the community exemplifies and communicates to the sufferer in a palpable way the meaning of the ministry of Christ and his offering of himself to die for us. It is communication because the community here is not simple behaving arbitrarily but is acting out of gratitude for what God has done for them in being incarnate in Christ and suffering for their sake. As such the community illustrates the steadfast disposition of God to love the sufferer even within the pained perplexity of suffering.

In the love we show each other, we model the love of Christ and encourage the suffering believer to reciprocate in love. When the believer loves as Christ loves, they begin to understand. Only the love of Christ can make sense of suffering. So we must do what we can to be present as a family with the suffering believer and avoid the extremes of swamping them or letting them get isolated.

Sometimes there is an answer to suffering but such suffering turns out not to be profound in itself. But when suffering is a mystery rather than a problem, then one realizes there can be no answer with respect to the sufferer – the answer is hidden in the wisdom of God. But rather than being the end of inquiry, it only makes our wonder deepen by turning its focus on the infinite God, the apprehension of Whom satisfies as the final end of our searching, while at the same time leaving us always yet to be satisfied. As Job says at the end,

> *"I had heard of you by the hearing of the ear,*
> *but now my eye sees you; therefore I despise myself,*
> *and repent in dust and ashes."* (Job 42: 5,6 ESV)

The sufferer is ready to let go of grief, not because he received what he demanded but because he now has a new orientation to God that is far more worth having than his original experience with God.

The solution to problems lies with us and our resourcefulness. But all mysteries lie with the hidden and obscure wisdom of God. Yet it makes a kind of sense that if we see that something is a mystery and neither a problem nor an arbitrary state of affairs, then there is a sense where it points to God as the only adequate ground of resolution. If no God exists, then there are no mysteries, only brute events of meaningless violence and no sense at all to suffering. Of course, that means there is no occasion to be perplexed by suffering either – stuff just happens. But the assumption that stuff just happens may be one of those false assumptions that gets undermined by real suffering.

In the second part of this book, we want to show that God has done much more than even this, that while secret things belong to God, He has yet made known some of His plans to us for our good.

VI. CONCLUSION: TO LIVE IS TO CHOOSE

Eventually, along side of the encouragements of the Body of Christ, the believer must decide whether to keep his or her trust in God. Some may fall back and say that they refuse to continue until God shows them something. Yet in this case, the believer must believe in order to see. Anger, grief, and acceptance are parts of a process, but how it goes is shaped by whether she resists or submits to God's will. There is a moment in suffering when the sufferer is faced with a moral decision to walk away or endure. This is the believer's responsibility and the church must be the community that models this responsibility. In this, we gently appeal not just to sympathy but also to the Christian conscience, just as God the Father is kind but also firm. When the suffering believer recovers their sense of there being a purpose to God's dealings with him or her, he or she completes the process by closing with God and submitting to His will. In this the Christian is like Mary, the mother of Jesus, submitting to Gabriel's message, "I am the Lord's servant. Let it be me to as you have said". By this submission, the believer once again owns his or her place in the peace of being in the will of God.

We work because God is at work. Just as Christ submitted to God without self-regard to the process of humiliation even to death on the cross, so believers must eventually choose to identify with the humiliation process going on in their lives. They must come to terms with their limited ability to understand God and His ways and be open to whatever they may be shown. In due time, they also share in Christ's exaltation and come to a real taste of their identity in Christ. Even if we are not suffering now, we must expect to suffer. The Scriptures make clear that all who call on the name of Christ must likewise be prepared to suffer as he did.

The position of someone who has completed a story with God is far better than it seems to him or her in the midst of that story. We would not be in a hurry to switch places with Job in the midst of his story. But we can also understand that he would not want to switch places with us at the end of it. A Christian who has walked with God in the dark is all the more radiant. He or she comes back with gifts for God's church. The greatest gift of all is the deeper joy that only comes with a pilgrimage through suffering. In this, the Christian also resembles Jesus, who is said to have endured the cross for the joy set before him. It is difficult when we suffer to see that there is a joy set before us but we must in word and life keep that joy before us and those who suffer.[14]

---

[14] See Peter Kreeft, *Making Sense of Suffering*, Charis Books, 1986.

4. The Problem of Faith and Science

Besides the problem of evil, another reason many find Christianity unconvincing is belief that Christianity conflicts with science, and more specifically that the history in the Bible conflicts with the phenomena of evolution. As described in Chapter 1, it is part of the modern plausibility structure that science is the paradigm of knowledge. Only what is measurable by scientific standards is worthy of assent. Since Christianity essentially involves claims to truth or to duty that seem not to be what may in principle be scientifically tested, including claims to miracles which although they ostensibly took place in history are not anything repeated or predictable from the study of nature, then it is unworthy of belief. Consequently, the priests of the modern age are not the prophets and theologians but the scientists. There is the belief that there is a conflict between science and religion, such as the issue often formulated in the press when discussing the various court trials over teaching creationism in the classroom. We can spell out the argument like this: since scientific knowledge is the only reliable knowledge, and since the content of Christianity is inconsistent with the content of science, then rationally we cannot accept Christianity as true.

I. REALISM IN SCIENCE AND ITS ALTERNATIVES

As we said, much commentary suggests that science is in a privileged place to speak from authority to various issues. In hearing this theme we need to be aware of some of the important developments in philosophy of science. I won't give an analytically refined discussion of this but I will try to cover the main themes.[15]

A natural presumption about science is that it is a rational discipline that brings us to the truth about nature, or at least closer and closer to the truth. If we think of this tendency as a viewpoint on science, we can capture that view in a couple of theses; one, science aims at true beliefs and the beliefs that are formed scientifically are either true or at least approximately true. And two, science is an enterprise that moves forward rationally. That is, reason can identify features in scientific theories that indicate their likelihood of truth, such as fitting well with the facts, internal coherence, economy of explanation, fruitfulness in guiding future research, experimental testability, ability to predict future or hypothetical outcomes, and like such. Call these "theoretical virtues" since if they are true of a theory then that is a reason for thinking that the theory is true rather than otherwise. So we can choose between rival theories by deciding which have the best combination of these features. So let's call the view of science that holds both of these claims scientific realism.

It is easy to think that at least most scientists are scientific realists about science. However, many things about the history of science make it difficult to be a rational realist. For example, in the past, theories that were accepted because they seemed to have a better combination of theoretical virtues were later established

---

[15] For a more detailed discussion of scientific realism and its alternatives, see J. P. Moreland, *Scaling the Secular City*, Chapter 7, Baker Academic, 1987.

to be false or thought to be false, while theories previously rejected have been later found to be true. Also, according to realism, science gets closer and closer to the truth. That can only be because the theory keeps getting adjusted to fit new discoveries. But there is no way to tell the difference between when a theory is being refined and when a theory is being replaced. Realism suggests that there is more refinement than replacement going on but there is no way to confirm this. And propositions are either true of false. There may not be any sense to make of saying that science could be "approximately true" (too fuzzy) and very little that could simply be said to be simply true.

There are many examples in history in which there was no apparent way to choose between rival theories. The most significant example of this was the comparison between the heliocentric theory of Copernicus and the geocentric theory held by the church at time of the Galileo trial. The trial concluded that while Copernicus' theory was certainly more economic, there were more anomalies with it that Galileo had not solved at the time. Given the apparent parity of explanatory value between the two at the time, science was not in a position to decide between them. Since the heliocentric theory seemed to fit better with a natural reading of Scripture, the church rejected Copernicus' theory until further evidence came to light.

Finally, quantum mechanics seems to be a thriving research program now, so it is seen as a case of paradigm science. But quantum mechanics does not seem to fit with a rational realist view of science. According to the Copenhagen interpretation, the state of a quantum particle is indeterminate between several possibilities and only becomes determinate to one possibility based on the observer of the particle, as if it were the seeing that makes it true. Dr. Schrodinger argued against this by a thought experiment. Suppose you made an invention that detects quantum particle radiation. If a quantum particle is detected, the machine activates a switch that releases a poisonous gas. And finally suppose you put this apparatus in a box with a cat and closed the lid. According to Schrodinger, if the Copenhagen interpretation is right, the cat is suspended between being dead or alive, being both and neither, until I look inside the box. Such a state would be self-contradictory. However, the phenomena at the quantum level lend themselves quite readily to the Copenhagen interpretation.

In general, the history of science is constantly either revising or replacing older theories which suggests that even today's theories will eventually be altered or replaced. Realism seems to explain the history of science but not any better or worse than the denial of realism.

Because of the difficulties facing rational realism, some philosophers have defended alternatives to it. One alternative, scientific nonrealism, denies that scientific theories are true or approximately true. This view rejects the idea that science aims at truth. Science is still a rational enterprise except that instead of aiming at truth it aims at something else like providing maps of the world that are more and more useful or predicting the most likely future experiences or simply capturing better how the world seems to us. Scientific nonrealism may be a possible way of viewing quantum mechanics, for example.

Another and more radical alternative is to deny both that theories are true or get closer to being true and that science is a rational discipline. Call this alternative Scientific nonrationalism. On this view, not only does science not aim at truth but it does not proceed rationally. According to this view, there is no reason to prefer one theory to a rival and such choices are thus not determined by intrinsic or evidential causes or by considerations like greater usefulness, but rather by social interests and institutions. According to the person most associated with this view, Thomas Kuhn, argued in his book on The Structure of Scientific Revolutions that instead of a gradual progress towards truth, the history of science displayed sudden reversals or scientific revolutions that were dictated primarily by interests invested in particular rival research programs. For example, it is plausible to think that the Galileo affair was driven by the vested interest the Church had in preserving its cultural authority, but also that those supporting Galileo had an interest in overthrowing that authority. The most extreme version of this view says that science is noting more than a social construction to help perform social functions that have nothing to do with the question of truth.

Which view to hold, whether scientific realism, scientific nonrealism, or scientific nonrationalism, is an open question for both Christian and non-Christian and one can find good reasons for holding to each view. For example, Christian philosophers Gordan H. Clark and Stuart C. Hackett defended particular versions of scientific nonrealism.[16] It is possible to be eclectic about which view to hold depending on the case. Just as one can be a skeptic about ghosts or flying saucers without being a skeptic in general, one can also be a scientific nonrealist about quantum theory while being a scientific realist about most anything else. The important thing to remember is that it is only where one decides the right approach to a certain field of science is scientific realism that one has to be concerned with reconciling science to other claims to the truth from other sources. If science is doing something else than asserting a truth claim, then there is no potential for contradiction, and therefore no conflict.

II. THE LIMITATIONS OF SCIENCE

As we saw, a premise of the argument that there is a conflict between Christianity and science is the belief that science is the paradigm of knowledge. There is a tendency to view science as the be all and end all of knowledge. However, there are ways in which it is clear that possibility of scientific knowledge cannot be considered self-sufficient. For example, if we take the claim of science to be that the only acceptable claims to knowledge are those that are scientifically established, then this would be self-defeating. This claim cannot be scientifically established. No experiment can tell us that only science can tell us the truth. Further, science cannot proceed without taking some propositions

---

[16] Gordon H. Clark, *The Philosophy of Science and the Belief in God*, Trinity Foundation, 1996 and Stuart C. Hackett, *The Reconstruction of Christian Revelation Claim: A Philosophical and Critical Apologetic*, Baker Book House, 1984.

for granted, such as that the five senses are standardly reliable. Science assumes a whole complex background of unquestioned assumptions in order to critically examine some propositions against evidence which are largely subordinate and kept out of view during the experiment. Assumptions about what things are taken as true about the field of study, about what count as the best kind of explanations in such and such kind of research, and about the reliability of the apparatus used in the experiment. Science cannot examine everything all the time. As Michael Polanyi argues, there is always an element of faith in science to make science possible.[17] If scientific reasoning is reasonable so are the other kinds of reasoning and belief formation that make science possible.

Furthermore, the claim that science alone is what should count as the only authority for knowledge often supposes that one can mark a clear boundary between what is and what is not science. But there are certain boundary issues where science slips away into traditional philosophical and theological territory. Two examples are cosmology and psychology. In cosmology, attempts to explain what went on during the beginning of the universe have led some scientists, like Stephan Hawking, to venture into philosophical territory. The theses offered on this level are the sort that admit of scientific experimentation but do raise questions of whether something can come from nothing. Also difficult to navigate is the transition between the physical

---

[17] See Michael Polanyi, *Personal Knowledge: Towards a Post Critical Philosophy*, University Of Chicago Press; Corr. Edition, 1974.

states of the brain and the qualities of subjective experience. Has science lost its way and become philosophy? The boundary is not clear. Finally, even science cannot ignore things that are not science but still taken to be true in other fields. An example is moral judgments. It is difficult for science to give an account of the truth that torturing infants for fun is wrong. But scientific claims cannot be inconsistent with it if it is true. Other examples include facts of history and aesthetic judgments.

From this we conclude that even where we decide that scientific realism is appropriate, science still relies on other kinds of reasoning to arrive at its best conclusions and is not self sufficient. Even if scientific knowledge is of great authority, the presuppositions of the faith are likely to be about those matters which are at the natural limits of science and where its authority comes to its limits. So it is possible that Christianity may have the same status as the necessary conditions of science and science may have to adapt its claims to be consistent with revelation.

III. OPERATION SCIENCE AND ORIGIN SCIENCE

Another view of the relation between science and faith is expressed by both religious leaders and scientists, like the late Stephan Jay Gould. He argues that there is no conflict between them since the cover wholly different areas of content and me-thods of determination. Gould calls his own statement of this view NOMA (Non- Overlapping Magistaria).[18]

---

[18] Stephan Jay Gould, *Rock of Ages: Science and Religion in the Fullness of Life*, Ballantine Books, 2002.

This is certainly better than thinking that science must be incompatible with religion and mostly for the reason that there are disciplines which seem independent of each other (Mathematics and Literature, perhaps). But supposing that Christianity is true, there are places where we would expect a divine footprint in the natural order, with respect to creation, providence, special revelation, or miracles, and this is especially true for those committed to the doctrine of the inerrancy of scripture. So the domains are not always expected to be non-overlapping and insistence on NOMA could be a way of excluding supernatural Christianity as a legitimate religious option.

In addressing this, I want to distinguish between at least two kinds of science. One kind of science studies the regular operations of nature, the natural laws of biology, chemistry, physics, astronomy, etc. Or another way of putting it is that this kind of science studies intermediate or instrumental causes in nature, where things effect other things but not without being effected by other things first. Call this Operation Science. This characterizes most standard sciences. In contrast another kind of science studies non-repeating and unique events in nature or studies effects which are the result of non-intermediate, not-instrumental causes like the actions of agents or unique events. Let's call this, Origin Science.[19]

One example of origin science is forensic science where the scientist is using scientific methods (genetics, ballistics

---

[19] Norman L. Geisler & J. Kerby Anderson, *Origin Science: A Proposal for the Creation-Evolution Controversy*, Baker Book House, 1987.

materials chemistry) to detect personal causes or when mathematicians study actuary reports to look for fraud. Another example is the Search for Extra-terrestrial Intelligence (SETI) project featured in Carl Sagan's book "Contact". Other examples of origin science might be cosmology, information theory, punctuated equilibrium, neuroplasticity, intelligent design theory, all projects which are taken to be, with different degrees of controversy, properly scientific and which make use of scientific methods but which aim at a singular cause rather than discovering a regularity of nature. The point is that if the "magisteria" or domain of science also includes origin science, then this could be a connection with a religion that sees God as acting in special ways in the natural order. We can see that NOMA would rule this out in advance.

One response to this would be to say that what now seems like a stable case of origin science will ultimately be fully explained by operation science. One way of expressing this claim is in the charge that origin science is guilty of the "God of the Gaps" fallacy. The idea of the God of the gaps fallacy is that whenever there is no obvious explanation for something that happened – whenever there is a "gap" in regular operational scientific explanation, God is always available to "plug the gap" as an explanation. However, later a more immanent and causally satisfactory explanation by natural causes is discovered and the God explanation is no longer necessary. This makes God's role in explaining the world ever decreasing, causing people to suppose that eventually all things for which God is given as the explanation will instead be explained by natural causes, which means that in the end God explains nothing and there is no reason to suppose he exists. In this light, the appeal to God is a "thought stopper", closing debate too early and preventing a more adequate investigation into nature.

Against this "God of the gaps" objection to origin science, we distinguish between explanatory gaps that are simply due to lack of further information and those gaps which are gaps in principle where we have positive evidence or reason to think that an operational explanation is not possible in principle. It is not because of what we do not know that we admit a gap in operational science, but because of what we do know and what we keep discovering that makes us think there is a gap is there. That such gaps may arguably exist is clear. An example is astronomer Robert Jastrow's discussion of Big Bang Cosmology, the strongly supported conclusion that the universe and space and time began with a great explosion of matter at a definite point, a conclusion that has frustrated many astronomers who presumed an infinite regular past operation of the universe.[20] The Big Bang is an example of a gap supported by science, as well as a case where appeal to a gap has won over previous appeals to operational explanations. While some may in such a situation still insist that we never give up looking for an operational explanation, usually by adding that the perplexity of not seeing how such an explanation is possible is only due to a lack of imagination, such a proposal is now much more contentious and disputable given the

---

[20] Robert Jastrow, *God and the Astronomers*, Readers Library, New and Expanded Edition ed., 2000.

evidence. Other examples of gaps could be the origin of life from matter and the origin of consciousness, intelligence, and choice in man.

While it seems that introducing a gap may put an end to operational investigation on the issue in question, it does not make the gap immune from investigation entirely. Origin science does not claim to be total or standard science. Operational explanation in similar and contiguous fields of science to the issue in question may overturn the gap in the self-correcting advancement of science. Just as one may choose reflectively whether a theory should be regarded from the point of view of scientific realism or nonrealism or nonrationalism, one may reflectively judge whether a case is best seen as a case of origin or operation science.

IV. ORIGIN SCIENCE AND CREATION SCIENCE

If there may be gaps, then origin science is a possibility. If so, then we could speak of a science of creation as a case of origin science. Various views going by the name of "creation science" have come under fire, in particular through being pursued in court rulings against the use of "creation science" or "Intelligent Design" in public school curricula. We won't address the issue of policy here.

But doesn't any idea of a science of creation involve an illegitimate intrusion of theology into the domain of science? In answering this, we want to take a modest view of the relation of theology to science. A strong view of the relation between creation and science would be to take the deductions of religious doctrine about natural phenomena or the interpretation of biblical literature concerning natural phenomena and call that "creation science". But it would be illegitimate to call this science because the conclusions have not been arrived at through the rational investigation of nature itself. A more modest view would be to allow theology to guide in developing hypotheses compatible with and suggested by doctrine but which are to be tested and supported only scientifically. Since the origin of a hypothesis is distinct from the support for it, the fact that a hypothesis finds its inspiration in theology should not affect its scientific status. Further, we want to say that whatever may be the obligation (say in the calling of a scientist who is also a Christian) from the side of theology, from the side of science, a scientist who allows theology to inspire his hypothesis formation is well within his scientific rights to do so. Finally, we also want to say that the domain of science itself is a stewardship under God and has its own prerogatives in distinction from theology that guide its pursuits, to which the Christian scientist is also obliged. While Christian scientists may consider how theology inspires hypothsis formation, it will not necessarily be the whole or even the main part of what they are to do for science.[21]

Still, some will object to even a modest conception of creation science. They will argue that God could not have any place in a properly scientific enterprise, since God transcends the

---

[21] See Abraham Kuyper, *Lectures on Calvinism*, William B. Eerdmans Publishing Company, 1943.

visible order of nature and the meaning of the concept of God could not be a proper object of scientific inquiry. For the same reason, statements about God are not scientifically testable or open to revision in the light of science. For these reasons, it is meaningless in any sense to speak of creation science.

But a scientific theory that refers to God is not for that reason unscientific. "God" is referred to in many disciplines in a non-religious way, particularly in thought experiments, along with similar concepts such as Maxwell's Demon. Also, it is not necessary to have a concept of God to know that there is something that exists that is responsible for an effect, such as the Big Bang or the presence of complex information in a cell, that could be what many people have in mind when the talk about God. We can scientifically infer the existence of a cause without being able to describe it.

Creation science is not in principle untestable. This complaint may have in mind the idea that statements are observable and therefore verifiable by science or they are not. In contrast to the view that a theoretical statement must be observable to be testable, it turns out that theories are confirmable in packages with other claims. For example, Neptune is a planet that was at one time beyond the range of our instruments, and was thus unobservable. However, it was shown to exist because of observed strange behavior in the planet Uranus. This was because of acceptance of other statements about gravity and mass that connect the evidence between the observed planet and the unobserved planet. Without the physics, the Uranus observations would not give evidence of Neptune. Similarly the statement

"God created the world" which is necessarily unseen could still find evidential support in the observed statement "DNA contains sufficiently complex information to produce a living organism" if we add theses such as that such complex information is extremely unlikely to arise spontaneously from prior physical causes alone, and that complexity of information and its efficient tendency to produce a specific object is analogous to intelligent and intentional causes. It turns out that whole sets of claims are confirmable rather than just individual hypotheses. In this way, unobservable claims like those about God may be open to evidential testing.[22]

It is said that creationists will hold on to their views come what may. But there is no need to expect that creationists need be any more or any less obstinate than non-Christian operation only scientists. It is part of the career of most theories to continue to pursue them even in the face of anomalous results. According to philosopher of science Imre Lakatos, theories are parts of larger research programs. Such programs develop around a hard and stable core of assumptions which are preserved if necessary by changing theories.[23] Further, theories are protected by many ad hoc hypotheses which are introduced to preserve the theory being dismissed out of hand from counter-evidence in normal science. This is often a prudent call because the state of play of the research may shift back to the theory as away from it. In this way what refutes a theory is not necessarily what rejects a whole

---

[22] Thom Notaro, *Van Til and the Use of Evidence*, Presbyterian and Reformed Pub. Co, 1980.
[23] Brendon Larvor, *Lakatos: An Introduction*, Routledge, 1998. See Figure 2 in Chapter 16.

research program. Creation science may be thought of as a research program in this sense, having a hard core set of assumptions and some ad hoc hypotheses to preserve the theories in question just as operation science does. Thus, the creation scientist and the operation scientist have the same problem of not being able to say in advance of experiments what would count as sufficient evidence for overturning a research program, but that does not rule out the conceivability that such evidence exists.

So it's possible that a creation science might be a good instance of origin science and thus good science.

V. SCIENTIFIC REALISM, OPERATION SCIENCE, AND THE BASIS OF NATURAL LAWS

We have been defending Christianity against the claim that it is incompatible with science. But while we are on the subject, I want to consider some features that contribute to the case for God. While it is possible for a Christian to take a position against a realist account of science on any subject, we want to allow that there may be some cases of science best described as requiring a scientific realist view. Given that origin science rather than operation science is really what is most controversial to most science-based critics of theism, we want to accept for the sake of the argument that there is some scientific realist operation science. If there is some legitimate scientific realist operation science, then what would make such a science true? This is to ask what would make scientific claims about natural regularities or laws true.

A natural law, like the law of gravity, is often expressible as a set of conditions. For example, according to the law of gravity, if I let go of my pencil, it will fall to the floor. If the law of gravity is true, then it is true even if I don't let go of my pencil. A common intuition is that if I believe something and that belief is true, then there is some state of things that "makes" my belief true and without which it would not be true. So what would make such a belief in the law of gravity concerning my pencil true?

One view says that so-called laws of nature are simply observed regularities, that the only thing that "makes" the law of gravity true is solely that in the past whenever we have noticed, the event of the pencil falling to the floor has happened to follow my letting it go. Apparent causation turns out to be simply correlation of events. However, most science could not be analyzed this way since no one could have seen all the relevant events billions of years into the past. This leads to scientific nonrealism about operation science. Also, much of science rather works with highly idealized thought experiments or rigorously defined lab experiments. So any mere regularity to us is just not available for notice.[24]

A realist answer is that what makes laws true are the dispositions inherent in the nature of things. A disposition is a property that something has that is not merely a potential for that thing but also makes it likely that the potential will be actualized in certain circumstances. An example of a disposition is some-

---

[24] This view was expressed originally by David Hume. (David Hume, *An Enquiry Concerning Human Understanding*, Tom L. Beauchamp, ed., Oxford University Press, USA, 2006).

thing like "being fragile" or "being freezable". We say that a piece of glass is fragile if it breaks easily when hit. But it is true of the glass that it is fragile even when nothing is breaking it. We say of water that it is freezable because if you put it in cold climate it turns solid. But that is already true of the nature of water, warm or cold. Dispositions are objective features of the nature of things that cause them to tend to do some things and not do other things. They make true hypothetical claims like if I let go of the pencil, it will fall.

Some will object that such an account is trivial. It sounds like I am saying that opium makes me fall asleep because it has somniferous dispositions, which sounds like saying that opium makes me want to sleep because it makes me want to sleep. However, the term is not trivial, but rather minimal. "Somniferous dispositions" is a term that refers to those features in opium that causes sleep. While that does not tell us anything about what those features are, it does tell us that they are. It indicates that there is such a ground for the disposition in the opium itself. Appeal to dispositions is not meant to be a complete explanation but to establish that which makes natural laws true.[25]

So a realist approach to natural laws would attribute their truth to the dispositions in nature of the things studied by science. But what this does is explain why certain states of affairs follow from an event rather than others. The subsequent way that things go is picked out by the nature of the things themselves. The Moon

---

[25] Edward Feser, *The Last Superstition, A Refutation of the New Atheism*, St. Augustine's Press, 2008.

seems to orbit the earth in a steady path rather than abruptly stopping or jumping up and down or shooting off to Jupiter at any given moment. The fact that certain states follow rather than others indicates that natural things have specific outcomes.

But it is puzzling that natural objects could have specific outcomes or ends when they are not conscious. Many would say that for us to call natural objects specifically directed is a mere projection of a human-like intelligence on what is not intelligent, like when we ask how the thermostat knows when to turn the furnace on, even though the thermostat really cannot be said to know anything. So for example, when we say that the purpose of the heart is to pump blood there is no assertion that the heart really is for anything but just that we cannot help but describe it that way. According to one approach, it is useful to us to describe the heart as we might describe a carburetor as a functional component of a car. We adopt a stance that deliberately projects a purpose or function until we finally get to the evolutionary history of how this material came to be here in this distribution, then discarding the concept of heart and its functions away as no longer informative and apt to mislead.

The problem with this approach is that it is clear that what makes something a heart, to stay with our example, is not that it has such and such an evolutionary history. It is clear that we can imagine many alternative histories that could lead to the coming into existence of hearts. Suppose God were to make a person from the dust of the ground so that he had all the same molecules as you have now. We would say that such a person had a heart even though it didn't have an evolutionary story at all. So being a heart does not mean having a certain natural history and there are hearts. It is hearts themselves that in part make the natural laws involving them true. This account extends to all other aspects of nature that are the basis of the truth of the natural laws that operational science seeks to discover.[26]

So natural but non-conscious objects are at least by nature specifically directed, whatever it is about them that directs them. However, to be specifically directed is to be instrumental to an end, to be in order to do something. And that can only be found in impersonal objects if it is arranged by an intelligent will that sees to it that such ends are realized. To see this, imagine a world where some plague has wiped out all humanity but left all technology and books and tapes and computers intact. Would cars still be anything more than scrap metal? Would books be anything more than ink blots on white pages? Their purpose would cease with humanity and they would be nothing but heaps of material stuff. We could say that they originally served a purpose for a humanity that once existed. But if humanity never existed, we could not conceive of these things being purposeful. We would have to say that there never were books or cars.

So if there are any things that have specific directedness, there must be intelligent will behind it. So if we can be scientific realists about natural laws, then there are natural things with specific directedness that make natural laws true. But natural laws have been true before humanity came into existence and they are true all through the universe where no humanity lives. So since

---

[26] Ibid.

you cannot have specific directedness without an intelligent will, there must be an intelligent will behind the universe of nature, which is what many people think of as God.

So either we are scientific realists about operation science or we are either nonrealists or nonrationalists about operation science. If the second, then there is no conflict between science and faith since science is not being taken to assert truth claims to possibly contradict Christian truth claims. But if the former, then operation science gives motivation to take God seriously, and so adds to the plausibility of Christian truth claims and creation science.

5. Encountering Other Faiths

When I was at a Christian college, I took a comparative religion course. One of the things we did was to take field trips to the centers of worship for other world religions in the city. On one trip, we were told we were going to a center for Vedanta Studies. It turned out to be a center for the Krishna Consciousness movement. We were given a tour of the facility and allowed to watch a ceremony of chanting. We also received a lecture about some of the distinctiveness of the doctrines of the movement.

At the next meeting of the class, we sat around in a circle and discussed our experiences at the center. This session turned into a collective session of doubting that descended to the point where most everyone began to wonder if there were any reasons for believing that Christianity was true. Before our visit to the center, I had read some useful material that warned about visiting such places because such doubt often happens. However, that did not prepare me for what actually did happen, and I think that the reason is that it had failed to account for the causes of such doubt.

This vertigo of doubt is an example of the "Rashomon Effect". The name is taken from Akira Kurosawa's film "Rashomon" in which the same event is described from four different points of view by four different witnesses. Each testimony is coherent but contradicts the other three. At the end, there seems to be no absolute perspective that leads to the truth.

This doubt that a Christian is apt to experience in encountering other worldviews is like experiencing the Rashomon Effect while looking at the world as a whole. It seems to support the objection that to say that there is only one truth or one way of salvation is arbitrary and arrogant. Why should Christians claim to have the only truth when there are so many different religions out there that provide a complete and adequate worldview for their adherents? Doesn't this cultural fact argue that each culture has its own way to God? Isn't it true that the only reason most people believe as they do is because they were born into it?

I. RELIGION AND TRUTH

What does it mean to say that a religion is true? We have to content ourselves with a few simple ideas in an informal discussion. Truth can be said of a proposition. The common sense way to think about this is that a proposition is true if it corresponds to a fact, a state of affairs that occurs at least at some time. So truth may be said of a proposition if and only if what it asserts is the case. Truth is often also attributed to a person. This can often be a term of approbation indicating that a person lives in a way consistent with their convictions, a person with integrity, worthy of trust. Or it is a way of saying that the person is the true object of worship and supplication as opposed to false claimants.

However, these two notions of truth are not often separated. Even if one speaks of a true person in either sense, propositional claims are involved. If a person is true to their convictions, those convictions can be expressed in propositions. If a person is the true object of faith and worship, which is a claim about them that can be expressed in a proposition, such as "Jesus is God". In either case, we do not refer to the true person without some description of him or her, such as "The man who gave us the law", which can be true or false. Even when dealing with a true person, some propositional truth claims are still involved.

To revisit a definition given earlier, we can say that a religion is true if and only if the propositions (doctrines, teachings) that are required to be believed to be a member of that religion are all true. As such, we may ask if these doctrines have the marks of truth. Are they inconsistent with each other? Do they make a coherent and comprehensive wordview? Do they fit the known facts? Can a person live by them morally and with integrity? Does depending on them involve a reasonable risk? And so on.[27]

With respect to the doctrines of various religions, if doctrines are true they need to at least be consistent. Are the various religions consistent with each other? There is the view that religion is like the story of the seven blind men and the elephant. One grabs the tail and thinks it's a rope. One grabs the trunk and thinks it's a snake. One grabs a leg and thinks it's a tree, and so on. According to these stories, each religion is a partial but adequate take on the same fundamental reality, even though that is not apparent to the various religious observers. On this view,

---

[27] Netland.

apparent contradictions are reconcilable, because the claims being made are only about one facet of a whole rather than the whole itself.

But it seems clear that some claims between religions are truly contradictory. For example, Western religions hold to the belief that we are substantial selves that maintain their identity over time, whereas Buddhism denies that there is any such self. It can't be the case that both claims are true. Christianity holds that God's glory is manifest in the death of Christ where Islam finds it abominable that God should allow Jesus to die. Some versions of Hinduism and Buddhism, such as Zen, insist on self-reliance against all help but other versions only provide for help from a special figure, such as Jodo Shin. There are several other such contradictions between religions so that we cannot simply say that they are all in some sense true. It is not possible for all religions to be all true about their essential doctrines, since they are not consistent.[28]

In response to this objection, some scholars have suggested that the beliefs of a religion are only the cultural husk of the religion and that religion itself is a state of piety in the subject toward the transcendent, that this state is what religion is and that this state is the same in all religious people while the cultural accretions are distinct and disposable. But this view seems to get the phenomena of the world religions wrong, many of which do seem to emphasize the so-called "accretions" as indispensable.

---

[28] Norman Anderson, *Christianity and World Religion*, IVP Academic: Rev Sub edition, 1984.

The fact is that it is difficult to capture the essence of religion in a common description. Judaism and Hinduism and Islam are religions, but what about Maoism? Maoism doesn't believe in God but neither does Buddhism. Judaism and Islam believe that God has spoken to man but even though Hinduism has sacred texts it sees itself as a religion based on reason. Rather than saying that we can define the essence of religion, it is better to say perhaps that religions have many "family resemblances" to one another and that to be a religion a movement must have a significant set of the possible features that characterize the main examples of it.[29]

Religions cannot simply be identified with the subjectivity of religious people. They are rich worldviews that combine various elements in different strengths. Each religion has a doctrinal facet, a narrative facet, an ethical facet, a mystical facet, a liturgical facet, a social facet, and a material (temples, statues, shrines, locations) aspect. These diverse aspects interact in a holistic fashion, providing the believer with an interpretation of the complexity of life to a substantially coherent degree. Among these aspects, especially the doctrinal aspect, are several that make truth claims. So we really cannot isolate the piety of a religion from its truth claims.[30]

---

[29] Paul Helm, *Faith and Understanding, Series: Reason & Religion*, Chap. 3, Wm. B. Eerdmans Publishing Company, 1997.
[30] Ninian Smart, *Worldviews: Crosscultural Examinations of Human Beliefs*, 3rd. ed., Prentice Hall, 1999.

II. RELIGION AND RELIGIOUS EXPERIENCE

One prominent religious ground for establishing religious truth claims is religious experience. Religions appeal often to the self authenticating character of their experiences as ground for the truth of the religion itself. Recently some brilliant philosophical work has shown that this may be sufficient.

One way to illustrate the credibility of religious experience is this: We take ordinary perceptual experience and sophisticated science to be a generally reliable guide to what is there. Religious experience is similar to perceptual experience. So we may take religious experience as reliable. In the case of perceptual experience, we are aware that many things can affect it (example: color blindness) but we take an "innocent until proven guilty" approach to our perceptual faculties. We also know that sometimes we see illusions (like a stick looking bent when placed in water, mirages) but we also have some criteria for distinguishing these cases from ordinary cases of perception. We also have methods for augmenting our perceptual faculties to see farther or smaller which extend our perceptual powers further. Finally, our ability to make sense of perception presupposes a certain set of background assumptions which the success of perception has given us no basis to doubt.

But it turns out that all these things may also be said of religious experience. Different religions involve an inner sense or a sense of Deity which seems to be consistent with itself and with other sources of knowledge. We are also free to take an "innocent until proven guilty" approach with this sense, which seems to be reliable. That sense can be cultivated by various methods and practices (like practicing the Presence of God). There is no reason to deny internal criteria that discerns genuine from dysfunctional sensation of God. And there are similar realistic assumptions that are involved with and are tested by religious experience. So it seems that religious experience is reliable in as much as ordinary perceptual experience is ordinarily reliable, by parity of reasoning.[31]

But here we have a problem. Because while this is true of Christian experience, it is also true of the Buddhist experience of Nirvana and of the Hindu experience of the Atman. It seems the two practices that are comparable to perceptual experience are comparable to each other. That makes all these various religious experiences apparently reliable. Yet based on their special experiences, the Christian affirms one thing and the Buddhist denies that thing, so that the two testimonies cancel each other out. Many say that even granting this, a person's own experience is a sufficient basis for grounding their own beliefs. You and someone else were at the same street corner and you see a clown walk by but the other says it wasn't a clown. If there are no reasons to think that your experiences are more or less reliable than the other person's, then you would be entitled to go by your evidence rather than have to submit to someone else's testimony. Still, if someone is in conversation with another and it comes down to comparing experiences, one will find a good argument for skepticism about these experiences if this is the whole story.

---

[31] Moreland.

However, religious experiences can be important as part of a cumulative positive case for one's own faith

This situation illustrates what went wrong in that classroom. Even college students can see the point of religious skepticism brought on by meeting sincere adherents from other faiths. This also makes sense of the arrogance charge against any religion that claims to have the truth, as if they had anything over and above what other religions have. This shows that negative apologetics (showing that objections to your faith do not succeed) is important but not sufficient. One must also try to give reasons why one's own faith is more reasonable to hold than alternatives (positive apologetics), a task we take up in the second part of this book. However, we can at least say at this point that it simply cannot be assumed that all religions are on a par with respect to the truth without examining them by the various tests for truth and credibility.

III. RELIGION AND RELATIVISM

Or can we? When we look at the phenomena of other great religions and admit that there is clearly a great deal of diversity among them, it occurs to us that many religions may be so different that they cannot even communicate with each other. This perception is pumped up by certain views coming from cultural relativism in anthropology. The idea is that though words may often seem to translate from one language to another, the cultural network of associations is so different for each culture that a word in its own cultural context cannot be said to truly translate into another language in another cultural context. Everything tends to get lost in translation. But this seems to be too strong and fails to do justice to the apparent evidence that translation often seems to be adequate.

Another sort of relativism is conceptual relativism; the idea that what counts as rational in a given culture depends on norms germane to that culture just as other kinds of values are relative to that culture. We had a taste of this in our discussion in the previous chapter of scientific nonrationalism in science - the view that there is no rational basis for choosing between rival explanations based on evidence or the quality of features of theories that make them better explanations of the evidence than others. On this view of culture, the standards that evaluate claims are different for each culture. There is no set of standards that are neutral between cultures so that claims of a religion compared against another can be impartially settled. Each culture holds its religion because by its own standards it is the most reasonable religion to hold. If that is true, then there is no basis for comparing religious claims to truth.

To see how this might be the case, we need to look at some examples of what might be criteria of evaluating truth claims, criteria which may or may not be accepted by different worldviews. One such criterion is logical consistency. A worldview must at least strive to be consistent since only in a consistent view may all the doctrines be true. However, comprehensive consistency is possible for more than one religion so that comprehensive consistency alone is not a sufficient test to decide which view is most true. Another principle is that explanations that make sense of more facts with the fewest sources of explanation are more reasonable than others. Suppose I leave an empty glass on the kitchen counter and come back and find it full of water. I might think that someone else in the house came in and filled it while I was gone. I might also think that a hundred people, each with a dropper, put a drop of water in the glass while I was gone. But I will think that the first explanation is more likely than the second because even though they both explain the full glass the first only posits one additional factor rather than a hundred.

Simplicity is more controversial than consistency, however, because even though it is more informative than consistency, there is often more than one sense in which one explanation can be simpler than another and these may rival each other. There are other criteria as well - predictive power, existential satisfaction, etc. - which all seem to appear to be good criteria for a good worldview when all other considerations are equal. However, different worldviews can adopt different sets of such criteria and even understand some of them in different ways, so that there is no agreement about the rules of the game of evaluating truth claims.

This view seems to assume that such evaluative criteria are givens in the culture or at least that their existence in the religious worldview is merely a by-product of that culture's history and that they thus determine what people in that culture believe to be the most rational beliefs to accept. The view does not seem to conceive of the possibility that such criteria can be revised or replaced from the feedback of ongoing interaction between the religion and the world of facts as experienced by members of that culture. Cultures that develop a desire to investigate and challenge their beliefs philosophically, ethically, or scientifically would need to be aware of their evaluative criteria and be open to revising or replacing them. In such cases, not only would a culture have criteria for holding which views they do but also reasons for holding the criteria they do.

This opens up the possibility that worldviews can be compared after all. While stating common criteria in advance to test religious worldviews must be ruled out, one may still evaluate another's religious worldview in relation to one's own by imaginatively entering into the other's worldview while inviting the other to imaginatively enter one's own. Then each person may compare the other's worldview and their own experiences. Does the other's worldview make as good or better overall sense of your history as well as the other person's or conversely? Are there puzzles that arise in one worldview but not so much in the other? By empathetic imagination one may yet find reasons for switching or not switching religions.[32]

So it is possible that there is a right combination of criteria, worldview beliefs, and facts that proves to be the one answer to understanding and knowing reality. Do we know that there is such a final solution by pure reason? No, we do not. But neither does the skeptic about positive religious apologetics know that there isn't such a solution. The only way to know is to keep on

---

[32] I am applying to religious relativism an approach that Alasdair MacIntyre applies to traditions of inquiry. (Alasdair MacIntyre, *After Virtue: A study in Moral Theory*, University of Notre Dame Press; 3rd edition, 2007).

examining our worldview in the light of new information and rival views. The skeptic may either respond by not pursuing such an examination, in which case he is in no position to talk, or the skeptic can make an inquiry of his own showing either that it is still not decidable whether we can find a final solution or not -- in which case, it still might be true that we can -- or showing that it is more reasonable to think there is no solution than that there is -- in which case the skeptic is no longer a skeptic and is positively defending a worldview of his own.

Thus it is possible that our beliefs are not arbitrary and our holding them is not necessarily arrogant if we can make a good case for them. Such a case does not have to be a philosophical demonstration, it can be sufficient if it is more like a courtroom style determination based on presentation of evidence. The rational certainty in Christianity can be the result of a cumulative case of mutually reinforcing evidence across various departments of understanding, including but not confined to science, history, philosophy, and religious experience.

Besides defending the possibility of criticizing religion from relativism, there is also the fact that religions do debate each other in practice. Just about every great religion has many a strong internal debate over different schools of thought and practice. For example, Chan (Zen) Buddhism claims to be the most pure form of Buddhism, while certain other schools of Buddhism say that it is not Buddhist at all. Buddhism itself was discovered in India where it was treated by Hinduism as a heresy. Also, religions have engaged in debate with outside religions. In particular, just as Christians can come into doubt when visiting other religious groups, members of native religions have vigorous responded to Christian missionaries by disputing their doctrines and defending the superiority of their own views. The picture that religious interaction should be characterized by a kind of non-confrontational dialogue is a recent phenomenon spurred by the rise of skepticism.[33]

IV. RELIGION AND JESUS

Returning to that doubt session at college again, we kept asking what, if anything, made Christianity true? Our professor replied that the question we needed to ask was what made Christianity unique. What makes Christianity unique is Jesus Christ. Jesus is the great fact that all religions must come to terms with and with which only Christianity deals with adequately.

One crucial distinction that sets Christ apart from other religious figures in other religions is his unique relation to the religion that carries his name. Gautama taught Buddhism but he was not necessary for the existence of Buddhist doctrine. Even Mohammed, though considered a prophet, was only the message bearer of Islamic revelation. But there could not be Christianity without Jesus and his death and resurrection on the cross. Jesus is the accomplished fact that brings about a new state of affairs, because he is uniquely the God-Man. We will get acquainted with the material about the history of Jesus and his resurrection, in order to introduce material into the pool of facts that one tests

---

[33] Anderson.

the reasonableness of one's religion by. But we claim that Jesus was a unique person, with a unique message, making a unique offering on our behalf with a unique ministry.[34]

V. CONCLUSION

In this section, we have not dealt with questions about what to think about other religions. It's clear that the Bible has much to say about the meaning of the existence of other religions and that this has to be brought to bear on the phenomena of the actual religions of the world. Whether religions, some or all, have their own access to divine truth, or are demonic deceptions, or modes of common grace, or a preparation for the gospel to other cultures – these are questions we have left untouched for the time being. But along the way, we have argued that the plurality of religions in the world does not imply that religious criticism is not possible. There can be a real prospect of knowing and showing that you know what the truth is about religious reality. While a superficial visit to other religions may plausibly pose the question of relativism and skepticism about religious truth, the prescription for doubt is a more aggressive engagement with the world religions, not a retreat from them.

---

[34] Michael Green, *But Don't All Religions Lead to God?*, Baker Books, 2002.

6. Is Faith Just Wishful Thinking?

I. INTRODUCTION: THE OPIATE OF THE MASSES

To begin our discussion, let's take a look at one more familiar objection. Isn't believing in God like believing in Santa Claus? Isn't it just a comforting thought we have because we cannot cope with some desperate situation, but we have no evidence for the notion of God?? Isn't religious and Christian belief just a type of wishful thinking?

The objection suggests that the reason people believe in God has nothing to do with reason and everything to do with either psychology or social pressure. This type of objection is certainly worth raising when there seems to be no rational motivation to hold a view or when all the evidence points against it. When proper reasoning fails to be the cause of a belief we start to look for another irrational source of explanation. So to say this of Christian belief assumes that there is no good reason to hold that Christianity is true. Of course, it's possible that what a person believes may be true but still held by the person for bad reasons, just as a person may have good reasons for believing something to be true which is yet false.

As a principle of charity toward each other, we do not want to propose that another person's reasons for holding a view are bad unless there is no evidence of any good reason or cause they may have for holding them. Everyone is innocent until proven guilty. We have been dealing with objections to the reasonableness of faith in the first part of our book to show they are inadequate reasons for thinking that Christian belief must be irrational. In the next part, we will give evidence for believing in Christianity. If we are successful in either part, there is no necessary reason to suppose the belief is wishful thinking by this rule.

Why think that religious belief might be wishful thinking? According to many atheists, religious people believe in God because they cannot cope with the nihilism that seems to be implied by naturalism, the view that there is nothing that exists except the physical and material world. If naturalism is true, there seems to be no objective purpose to life and to human life especially. There is no ultimate origin and no end that anything is for. Further, there is no free will and no moral responsibility, because human choices are simply events in nature that are either necessitated by the past events and the natural laws or because they are indeterminate and not really under anyone's control. There are no moral truths since there is no event that is by nature oriented to an end. Further there are no persons as rational agents. Human beings are essentially a network of interacting black boxes. Love then has no meaning since humans are not ends in themselves.

Our surest guide to happiness has to be by reconciling ourselves to absolute despair, as Bertrand Russell put it.[35] Many find this unacceptable. So to avoid it, they brainwash themselves with religious beliefs, which are essentially superstitious, to keep them from facing the truth. Also, it is difficult for society to

---

[35] Bertrand Russell, "A Free Man's Worship", 1903.

facilitate itself and its interests if people are desperate, so institutions encourage the fiction of religious beliefs. Thus, as Karl Marx suggested, religion is the opiate of the masses.

This does sound plausible enough to suggest that it may in fact explain the religious beliefs of some people. But does being aware of the implication of meaninglessness from naturalism and the uncertainty in the grounds of religious belief necessarily mean that faith must be just a projection?

Even if we may not have seen any compelling reason to decide that Christianity is true, it still may be rational to believe it. Suppose I made a bet with you: Give me a quarter and I'll flip it. If it lands on heads I'll keep it but if it lands on tails I'll give it back along with another quarter. Would you take the bet? You might for a lark - it's only a quarter. But if we were talking about betting $1000 on a double or nothing coin flip, you might decline - it's too much money to risk even on an even bet. However, what if I asked you to give me a quarter to flip and if it came up heads I would keep it but if tails I would give it back plus $1000. In that case, you might even think that it would be crazy not to take the bet. That is, even though the outcome is uncertain, it is reasonable to take the bet and not taking the bet is so unreasonable that it would violate a duty to live rationally. Suppose I asked for two quarters and said that I would only give them back if they both came up tails, but if they did I'd also give you $1000. You would still be crazy not to take the bet even though the odds are against you because the payoff is so big relative to the risk.

What then about belief in God? If God exists, then there is meaning to life and nihilism is false. This has implications for the value of this life as well as implications for the plausibility of a life beyond this life. But if naturalism is true, then life is meaningless and we should just fill the time as best we may. But which is true? If we knew, we could simply dismiss the matter and go with what we know, but many are unable to decide which is true and think that the case for God is moot. But what if I made a bet with you? You can either believe that God doesn't exist and live for the moment, or you can believe that God does exist and live this life focused on a purpose and with hope for the next life. You can't for all practical purposes simply suspend judgment, since as long as you live you are just living for the moment anyway, so it is just the same as believing that the world is meaningless. Now if God does exist, then your reward in this life is great and there is something to hope in the next life, if you act on belief in God. If God does not exist and if you do not believe in God, then even in despair you can still take advantage of the ample salad bar of life, including the items forbidden to the faithful.

But if you believe in God and there is no God, you may have gone so far as to sacrifice yourself on the pyre of martyrdom but all you have missed out on is more days of trips to the salad bar, because if God does not exist life is just sound and fury signifying nothing. But if you don't believe in God and God does exist you will have missed out on the greatest fulfillment possible, because then life will be the great probation and the great vocation of humanity and yourself. So it seems that believing in God is a lot like betting a quarter on getting a thousand dollars - something that is reasonable to do even if uncertain and thus not an irrational projection. Some may disagree with the assignments of value to each part but the way we have assigned them is not surprising. Even if we think that God is somehow intuitively more likely not to exist that still might not alter faith as a reasonable choice anyway, since that would be like the case of betting that two or more quarters will come up heads. And having granted that God exists and thus that the world is intelligible, meaningful, moral, and personal, we can then ask which religion is the most reasonable on this assumption.[36]

However, whether God can adequately account for a meaningful life to make our above gamble sufficiently reasonable may depend on what we think God is. But here the classical arguments for God's existence can help us form either a partial essential or functional concept of God without appealing to some prior religious background even if we suspend judgment about whether such arguments prove that God exists. For example, we may conceive of God as the greatest conceivable being in the sense that we think of God as the adequate source of the maximum of excellence, an infinitely perfect necessarily existing being. Such a being could create a meaningful universe.

Further, a believer may even grant that belief in God does arise because of a sense of need. There may be more of an analogy here between the need for God and the need for food than there is between a need for God and a need for faster than light

---

[36] William James, "The Will to Believe", 1896. For an explanation and illustration of James argument, see John G. Hartung, "The CPU Has Its Reasons", *Anime and Philosophy: Wild Eyed Wonder* (Popular Culture and Philosophy), Josef Steiff and Tristan D. Tamplin eds., Open Court, 2010.

space travel. The second is more of a hypothetical need given that we want to travel in space. But the first is a natural and essential need, the stomach exists to digest food. Hunger suggests that there is food somewhere even if one starves to death here and now. But wanting to travel in space does not imply faster than light travel is possible. Categorical needs, as opposed to hypothetical needs, imply the existence of the object - there is food somewhere. If our need for God is existential and not just instrumental, that is a reason for believing that God exists. And it seems that man really is homo pietas. Religion is in his nature because only in the secular west do we find humanity trying to live without religion.[37]

II. THE MEANING OF LIFE

An objection to the above is that we don't need God to live meaningfully. We can have a meaningful life without God. Let's take a closer look at the question of meaningfulness.

The question of the meaning of life can be asked at several different levels. (1) Is my individual life meaningful? (2) Is humanity meaningful? (3) Is the history of the whole universe meaningful? Different views will give different sets of answers. (See Figure) (A) NNN: If the answer to all three questions is "no", this is the view of total nihilism and of total despair. Life has no meaning whatever. (B) YNN: It is only possible to answer "yes" to the first question. This is secular humanism. Life only

---

[37] C. S. Lewis, *Mere Christianity*, Macmillan, 1960.

has as much value as you invest in it. This is also creative relativism since you determine what does count as meaning for your life by inventing your own values. But there is no fact of the matter about which values are good. What makes values good for you is the fact that you chose them for yourself, whether it is serving the starving in Calcutta or killing an old lady because she's a waste to society.

The third option is (C) YYN: A higher view is that even though there is no God, there are objective facts about value and morality that are not merely postulated or constructed by us. They are facts about nature but ones which have their own intrinsic ends and thus can be true reasons for making choices that give life meaning. Finally (D) YYY: The view that there is a cosmic purpose that includes all of universal history as well as us and the whole human race. On this view not only are there objective values and persons, there is also a purpose to history and a final reckoning of justice. Not surprisingly, a theistic view embraces meaning on all three levels.[38]

Is there a meaning of life for…				
	(A)	(B)	(C)	(D)
…me?	No	Yes	Yes	Yes
…Humanity?	No	No	Yes	Yes
…the Cosmos?	No	No	No	Yes

Figure: Meaning of Life Questions

---

[38] Moreland.

Of these options, only the first one denies any meaning at all to life. So it seems that one could hold a view that affirms a meaning to life at some level without holding to belief in God. But I want to suggest that not all these positions are explanatorily stable as worldviews and that they create tensions except the NNN and the YYY views. With regard to (B) YNN, it seems that this view does not really achieve escape velocity from total nihilism. One may behave any way one likes but there is no real difference between one kind of behavior and another. It may be said that the morality of such behavior is only the expression of the feelings of the subject, of which there is neither an accounting nor a basis.

A film that may illustrate the failure of this kind of view is Apocalypse Now, a film based in part on Joseph Conrad's story "Heart of Darkness". In the film, the protagonist is a military assassin who is assigned to take out one of the Army's own colonels who has gone off the ranch. At the assignment meeting, a tape of the colonel's voice is played where he talks about dreaming of a snail crawling along the edge of a razor blade and surviving. This image depicts the predicament of being a rational choosing being in a world without true values. One is faced with choices but has no criteria for making them, so the rational person just bluntly makes them and the authentic person makes them beyond convention. This is just a return to affirming nihilism. Further, we can see how this is really the heretical imperative view that we discussed in Chapter 1.

That is not true of (C) YYN. There are facts about values so one is not left to capriciously decide what to declare valuable.

However, the idea of objective values without an ultimate framework of meaning is puzzling. The brute existence of values in a world ultimately without purpose is unlikely. Such values would be more likely in a world created by God. Further, to postulate them without the background of theism would make it difficult to explain why it is rational for us to follow after objective values rather than live some other way. Without God to reward righteousness in the afterlife, the sacrifices that might be required by living by these values would make it less reasonable to do so. Then the objective value would become pointless in practice.

So it seems the most rationally stable options are either NNN nihilism or YYY theism. But the problem of nihilism is that it is unlivable. We cannot conscientiously act in a nihilistic world since all action is characterized by an end, and in such a world there could be no rational consideration for ends. Some have argued that this is not a problem. Even if reason were to tell us that nihilism is true our lives are governed by habit and custom, rather than consideration and reason. We just do what we do because of our culture. This however, ignores the real drawbacks of adopting such an attitude that are now creating problems for society. While we are not arguing that creative relativism is incompatible with being a good person, there are many ways in which this mindset can reasonably be connected with certain social deficits. For example, while community is often said to be worthwhile and important for conversation, the view that there is no objective purpose for individual human beings makes attaining community much harder. If everyone is under the description of being purposeless, there is not much incentive to work together.

This feeds the deterioration of civil society that seems to have caught everyone's notice.

Also the lack of a significant purpose in nihilism or creative relativism means that people tend to have no moral strength or energy to endure and no framework that makes sense of suffering. Reason is able to recognize some formal norms of conduct but the great accumulation of a moral tradition is undermined. The trans-generational testing of a way of life is unavailable in principle, so there is no adequate moral guidance or inspiration. This even effects the ostensive values that the Heretical Imperative view seems to have because even science, technology, and democracy requires well formed habits that nihilism lacks reason to support. Finally, the Heretical Imperative view seems to provide no vision for the future even though it seems to create the sense that the future is well nigh manageable. There is no reason to procreate future humans, why bring them into a meaningless existence? So though technology has been brilliant in producing new machines and services, nihilism has not nurtured either the will or the good judgment to use them.[39]

In the film, "Serenity" space travelers come to a planet where the Interplanetary Government has colonized by terraforming but also has doctored the atmosphere with a chemical to dampen the aggressive tendencies of the humans who live there. When the travelers get there they discover that everyone has dropped dead from lack of a will to try. In a way, nihilism is a

---

[39] Michael Novak, *No One Sees God: The Dark Night of Atheists and Believers*, Doubleday Religion; First Edition, 2008.

similar kind of atmosphere except that under it what is dampened is the disciplined energy that maximizes human potential in science and culture while curbing destructive impulses. It is an agent that is not merely passive but also aggressive in its tendency.

All this suggests that we are made for cosmic meaning and that our need for God is rooted in our nature as humans.

III. TRAUMA OF HOLINESS

Many have argued that the characteristic feature of religious experience is that the object of worship is high and lifted up, a mystery both terrifying and fascinating. Think for example of the book of Isaiah, chapter 6. In the beginning of the chapter, the prophet tells of an encounter with God in the Temple, surrounded by the angels and all singing "Holy, Holy, Holy". In the face of such a Presence, Isaiah declares that he is becoming "unmade" and that he is aware of his sinfulness and that of his people. If God is a projection, God is not what we would expect a projection to be. The concept of God in the Judeo-Christian tradition is not that of a Santa Claus type of figure, but a terrifying figure. In fact, rather than being something that someone might project, it seems that God provides an explanation for why someone would want to project a Godless universe.

Paul's development of the rejection of God by non-believing nations in Romans 1:18 and following seems to illustrate this. The decline described in Romans 1 can be understood in the psychological categories of Trauma, Repression, and

Substitution. According to Paul, the existence, greatness, and terribleness of God is clearly seen in his creation, so as to make humans without excuse. The vividness of God's majesty even as evident in nature is traumatizing and makes men want to escape. As a result, they do not acknowledge God or regard Him in anyway whatsoever, as if "God is dead". This is repression. Finally, men pursue the worship of other gods based on created things as alternatives to God; substitution.[40]

There may be some supporting evidence for this in some of the more candid things that atheists themselves say. Bertrand Russell explained that his turn to despair was in part due to escape from the "Puritan" concern over self-examination for sins. With even greater candor, atheist philosopher Thomas Nagel said that he thought what motivated philosophers to embrace such counter intuitive views about materialism and relativism is that they are driven by, as he put it, "fear of religion". He states that he himself has this fear. It is not just that he thinks that theism is not rational but even that he would hate it if it turned out that there was an Absolute God who could simply tell you what to do. At least some atheists admit that they find God traumatizing.[41]

The difficulty with suggesting that someone holds a religion or a worldview because of psychological need rather than for good reasons is that it opens the door for them to put the shoe on the other foot. This is one reason why it is important to observe

---

[40] R. C. Sproul, *If There is a God, Then Why are there Atheists?*, Tyndale House, 1988.
[41] Thomas Nagel, *The Last Word*, Oxford University Press, USA, 1997.

our principle of charity and assume innocence until guilt is established.

IV. GESTALT SWITCHES AND THE ROLE OF THE HEART

But if that's true, why do we hear that even some Christians do not see God revealed in nature, as a Christian leader once admitted to me. That God is seen in nature is crucial because on the bases of this the apostle Paul holds the lost from every nation responsible for their sin. How then can God fail to be recognized? The provisional answer is that there is some psychological repression mechanism that brings about the denial of the plain truth. If the truth is repressed, how does that mechanism work? We can only make a suggestion. Consider this illustration:

These images illustrate the phenomenon of "gestalt switching". It is possible for perception to synthesize the data in the picture into two alternative ways of making sense of it. This leaves the meaning of the picture ambivalent. Also, note that when we see the drawing as a duck we cannot see it as a rabbit and vica versa. Thus to see both we have to alternate from one perception to the other. The ability to do this is called gestalt switching. We can imagine a form of mental illness such that the person who has it can only see the duck and is not aware that there is anything else in the picture.

What is true of perception is analogous to worldview perspectives. The worldview we adopt synthesizes everything and creates a particular perspective. Adopting an alternative worldview will create a rival perspective. While we are embracing one perspective we will not see the world in terms of the other. Worldview perspectives determine plausibility structures. They shape what we judge to be plausible (and predict when we will either give or receive blank stare arguments as we saw in chapter 1). Worldview perspectives are not just shaped by perceptions but also beliefs and values.

So I suggest that the mechanism that makes suppression possible is when a worldview's plausibility structure fixes the setting of a gestalt switch. This makes the world seem like a naturally godless place for one holding a naturalistic or nihilistic worldview. As a result, the switch is wired down to the naturalist position. The pervasiveness of naturalism explains why even Christians born and educated in our culture find it difficult to experience what Paul is talking about when he refers to the immediate sense of God's power and divinity in the things He has made. Paul in Ephesians speaks of non-believers having been hardened in their hearts and as being insensible to divine truth. One of the aims of apologetics is to motivate the invitation for the non-believer to flip the gestalt switch and taste and see that the Lord is good.

Finally, whether we are talking about avoiding nihilism or avoiding God, these questions show that reason is not alone in evaluating the rationality of a worldview or religion. An important role is played by emotion and character as well. Some will respond by saying that such "matters of the heart" have no place in objective thinking, but it may be that having a certain character contributes to reliable belief formation while another is detrimental to it. Rather than emotions and character being a source of relativism, having a certain character may be the cure for relativism.[42]

V. CONCLUSION: REASON AND THE SPIRIT

Since the wishful thinking objection can be turned against the atheist, it is probably not a good thing for the atheist to bring up. It is better to take it off the table.

However, we should not forget the important lessons from this, especially the role of gestalt switches and perspective. Adopting a perspective is a choice that may have costs such as losing a profound sense of God's presence in the World. We

---

[42] William J. Wainwright, *Reason and the Heart, A Prolegomenon to a Critique of Passional Reason*, (Cornell Studies in Philosophy of Religion), Cornell University Press, 2006.

cannot make a fully considered choice without confronting the full spectrum of our attitudes.

While the role of the heart might cause discouragement for the unbeliever, it provides confidence to the believer who understands that the Holy Spirit must be at work in people's hearts before they will be able to see and be reasonably persuaded that Christianity is true. While the Christian apologist is using reasons and evidences to respond to objections and make the case for faith, they are grist for the effective working of the Holy Spirit in the heart of the unbeliever. The preparations of the defender go hand in hand with an absolute dependence on God.

7. Questions and Counter Questions

I. CHRISTIANITY AND FALSIFICATION

After listening to our previous responses, a keen agnostic may begin to wonder if there is anything we won't say in response to objections. There is an important sense in which they are right to be concerned. A position that in principle cannot be refuted ought to be rejected. This is the problem of falsification.

The importance of falsification in science was raised by Sir Karl Popper.[43] In the logic of deductive reasoning, one of the necessary features of a good deductive argument is called validity. Any argument from premises to conclusion is valid when the conclusion must be true if all the premises are true. For example, suppose my car is parked outside of the garage and not under a tree or canopy. So if it rains then my car will get wet. Suppose it is raining. Then I conclude that my car is getting wet. This conclusion necessarily follows from the two premises, that if it rains, then my car will get wet and that it is raining. It cannot be the case that the premises are true and it is false that my car is getting wet. And so this argument is valid, however uninteresting.

The premises do not actually have to be true in order for the conclusion of an deductive argument to follow logically.

---

[43] Karl Popper, *Conjectures and Refutations*, London: Routledge and Keagan Paul, 1963.

However, a deductive argument cannot be a good argument if it is not a valid inference. For example, suppose again that my car is still outside the garage as described before and also that it is getting wet. Does it follow that it must be raining? No, because I could be washing my car instead. So an argument from the premises that if it rains my car is getting wet and that my car is getting wet to the conclusion that it must be raining is not valid, because it could be that the premises are true but the conclusion is false. The premises do not logically guarantee that the conclusion is true. The first argument is a form of valid reasoning. The second is a form of invalid or fallacious reasoning.

But Popper observed that the reasoning typically used in scientific experimentation is fallacious in the same way as our example. A scientist can be thought of as observing some phenomena of the natural world, like reproduction in cells or orbits in comets, and asking about the cause. In answer, the scientist suggests a hypothesis. But in order to test the hypothesis, the scientist asks what detectable changes would occur if the hypothesis is true. The scientist decides that certain effects would occur under certain conditions that can be created in a laboratory if the hypothesis is true. Let us say it turns out the scientist is able to see those effects. Does that mean the hypothesis is true? The would-be scientist aims to deduce from the premises that if the hypothesis is true then this effect can be produced and that this effect is produced the conclusion that the hypothesis must be true. But that is the same kind of fallacious reasoning that concluded that it was raining because my car is getting wet. So if science proceeds by the experimental confirmation of hypotheses about the cause of natural phenomena it seems the whole enterprise rests on fallacious reasoning. How can that be when we seem to see science making such real progress?

Popper's answer was that science actually proceeds not positively by confirming hypotheses but rather by refuting rival hypotheses. Suppose my car is parked outside again like before but this time it is not getting wet. Since it could not but be getting wet if it were raining, I conclude that it must not be raining and this is a valid inference to the conclusion. In a similar way, we can validly conclude that certain hypotheses are false. If some effect in a laboratory would be the case if a certain hypotheses were true, but the effect does not occur, then we conclude that the hypothesis is not true. This is a valid argument and not fallacious. So Popper suggested that science actually progresses by refutation rather than by confirmation.

While Popper's view is not the last word on this subject, it does illustrate the attractiveness of falsification as a criterion of science. Theories are good theories if they are open to being falsified. However, hypotheses are not necessarily straightforwardly refuted by counter evidence. They may be qualified by adding limits to the conditions under which they are supposed to apply. This may be done a little without straining plausibility, but if a theory winds up having "too many" ad hoc limits, it may be better to just give up on the theory. But some theories may not be open to falsification at all. Such theories, Popper said, were not science but "metaphysics", theories that make no difference to the facts or the way the world might be. Such theories may be true but they also would be trivial.

II. CAN CHRISTIANITY BE SHOWN TO BE FALSE?

But many critiques of belief in God claim that theology must also be "metaphysics", a set of claims that are in principle incapable of falsification. This means that Christianity can only be accepted on faith. It has nothing to do with reasoning or the world. This is because it is not open to falsification in principle.

Antony Flew (before he became a theist himself) posed the issue this way. Suppose two persons came upon a garden-like arrangement of flora in the woods. One says that there must be a gardener, the other doubts it. So they decide to test the thesis by laying out traps and setting alarms and spying on the garden in hiding. But no one appears, no traps trip, no alarms go off. Still the one insists there must an invisible, intangible, super smart gardener that avoids getting caught. But the other asks, "What's the difference between your super gardener and no gardener?"[44]

As Flew put it, some propositions can be killed by inches and can die the death of a thousand qualifications. This illustrates what happens to the plausibility of a hypothesis when it gets qualified by too many conditions. It seems that some claims can be reduced to meaninglessness this way. Is that true of Christianity? One problem is that according to the Christian faith, the world is God's creation but that God created the world freely. It was God's own choice to make the world, which means he might not have made the world. So it seems that God exists no matter whether the world exists or not, and also no matter how

---

[44] Antony Flew and Alasdair MacIntyre, *New Essays in Philosophical Theology: Library of Philosophy and Theology*, SCM Press, 1955.

the story of the world goes if it existed. That seems to imply that the existence of God is compatible with any state of affairs and so nothing can show that the existence of God is false.

Further, it might be said that since Christians do not just believe in an all powerful God but also a good God, the thesis of a good God might be refuted by the existence of evil in the world. Yet we have seen in Chapter 2 that whatever might be considered a potential case of unjustified evil could always be considered due to the limitations of our own understanding. Finally, would not Christians say that it would be sinful to think that God could be shown to be false? Would not the admission that God was open to falsification just mean to doubt whether God is real? For all these reasons, the agnostic may think that there is no reasonable expectation that Christian theism would be open to be falsified, and thus must be otiose.

Strikingly, the Bible's attitude toward faith is one that is open to testing and falsification. God invites people to test him on various occasions. Moses is given various signs to show the Israelites and Pharaoh that he comes with God's authority. Elijah pits God against the Canaanite deities in a sacrificial showdown in which God sets fire to a sacrifice soaked in water. A biblical prophet was not to be believed if the prophecy failed to come to pass as the prophet said. Jesus demonstrates his authority by performing striking healings. The apostles in the history of Acts appeal to what the crowds and leaders have witnessed to attest to what they say. The apostle John exhorts the church not to believe every "spirit" but to test the spirits to see if what they say is true (1 John 4:1). It does not seem that the Bible would necessarily approve of construing its message in such a way as to make it immune from genuine criticism.

We can and must distinguish between the questions of whether evidence against God's existence is conceivable as a logical possibility and whether a gracious and good God exists. The first is a question of whether we can have evidence for or against God as a matter of reasoning and justification of beliefs. The second is a question about what is really the case no matter what we can or cannot think. The belief that God really exists and that everything in creation reflects his glory and goodness is not inconsistent with the belief that it is conceivable that certain evidence would prove that God is false if such evidence were obtained. According to Christianity, the resurrection of Christ was a fact planned and settled from all eternity to all eternity. Yet if someone produced the dead body of Jesus, then Christianity would be false. The Christian can consistently affirm both.

However, the issue of qualifying a thesis to deal with counter-evidence makes it difficult to say in advance of evidence what would be necessary and sufficient features of something that would count as decisive falsification. Since this turns out to be an issue that faces many theories in science, the objection that the Christian does not have in hand the precise formula of what would make Christianity false cannot be fairly applied only to the Christian. All research programs face anomalous data that do not easily fit the theory, but this does not yet indicate that the theory is not really closed to falsification.[45]

---

[45] Larvor, Lakatos: An Introduction, 1988.

In reply to Antony Flew, Christian philosopher Basil Mitchell gave a counter-example to Flew's gardener story. Imagine you are fighting with the French Resistance and while in the trenches, you meet a person whose presence alone commands respect and authority - a person you feel has heroic integrity you can trust immediately. He tells you that he is the Leader of the resistance and not to worry, for he has a plan for winning the war.[46] As the days go by, you and your comrades catch sight of the Leader from time to time. Sometimes he is seen leading the resistance fighters to victory over the Nazis and everyone cheers. But other times he is seen leading the Nazis against the resistance fighters and beating them. Your comrades say "He betrayed us! Give up on him!" But you think, "No, surely he has a plan and this apparent betrayal is really part of the path to victory for the resistance." You are willing to give the Leader the benefit of the doubt under the circumstances.

The crucial thing here is not that you will defend the resistance leader no matter what. Rather, you are not able at the time to specify under what conditions it will be clear to you that the Leader is betraying you. Thus, it is not necessary for the conditions of falsification to be explicit for you to have a rational confidence in a thesis. This applies in the case of the problem of unjustified evil. It is conceivable that something may happen that would count for you as unjustified evil even if now you could not clearly say what they would be.

---

[46] Flew and MacIntrye, 1955.

However, in the second part, we are going to offer arguments as metaphysical demonstrations of God's existence. If successful, or even plausible, they provide compelling reasons for believing in God that does not depend on falsification. We will also argue that one may have more direct knowledge of God that gives reason not to expect falsification. If either is true, then it would not be logically conceivable that God be open to falsification. However, we are still open to the possibility that our reasoning could be shown to be mistaken.

III. IN RESPONSE TO ALL YOUR OTHER OBJECTIONS

But I have a larger point to make than this. We most certainly have not covered all the possible objections to Christian faith. But in the practical experience of many who come to faith in Christ, it is often the case that they do not have all their questions answered. They remain patient regarding certain issues that will be answered in due time or that seem no longer significant reasons to withhold belief. For example, many come to Christ before they get the virgin birth or biblical authority settled.

We see the same in science. As was said, often a theory raises many difficult questions and anomalous cases, but this is not enough to discourage scientists to accept it as the dominant research thesis for their science. The explanatory and predictive merits weigh against the difficulties. And there are no clear criteria for when this occurs yet it seems to be paradigmatically a case that counts as rational to accept.

The same is true in the Gospel. In the Gospel witness, the non-believer encounters the person and work of Christ and this positive exposition becomes the central basis for assessing the worth of his objections. It is possible that what convinces a person to take Christianity seriously is not a reply to any specific objection, but a genuine grasp of the picture of Christ in the gospels, just as the partisan is impressed by the resistance Leader. Our most important apologetic is an adequate, accurate, and passionate proclamation of Jesus Christ. The apologist's main function is to be a martyr, a witness who simply says, "Come and see!"

IV. RAISING OBJECTIONS TO OTHER PLAUSIBILITY STRUCTURES

Returning to our discussion about plausibility structures in Chapter 1, the question is: How do we do that in our modern context? As we have seen, we are up against a plausibility structure that is preset and prefixed, against which all of our claims seem weird, extravagant, and even cruel. They do not seem to see the cruelty inherent in their own point of view. Modernity allows only for naturalism, atheism, preference satisfaction, and scientism. On this view, Christian supernatural-ism overtaxes credulity. Further, modernity is not willing to take any ideological risks for the sake of not missing out on any greater truths. It is happy with the bird in the hand of today's creature comforts rather than give them up to search for a higher purpose that might not exist as far as science can tell. The authority of modernity is enhanced by science and research as fields that display the competency of those gifted for the discovery and application of the knowledge of instrumentality of nature, much as Chinese culture would venerate Shaolin Buddhism because of the proficiency of its martial arts.

So we need a strategy for opening the way to presenting the Christian message to a generation without ears to hear it, insofar as that depends on us. We are like spies or double agents penetrating the fortress of the enemy and trying to find ways to lead them into captivity through their own perspective and resources. The idea of making intermediate connections from within a sinner's point of view to the point of view of the gospel is not illicit but part of the equity of rhetoric. It is also done in the Scriptures in various ways, especially by the prophets. We see it in how Nathan the prophet gets past David's defenses about his sin with Bathsheeba and Uriah by using the parable of the poor man and his lamb (2 Samuel 12). We also see it in the ministry of Hosea when God told him to marry a prostitute to bear witness against Israel (Hosea 1). Jesus in his earthly uses miracles and parables to the crowd because of their sinful unwillingness to follow Him. In all these cases, we see God working around the defenses of unbelief in order to put his witness where it will be seen and heard.

Let us call any attempt to orient a person from within his or her point of view to see the Gospel "pre-evangelism". Pre-evangelism can take many forms and invites creative brainstorming, especially in the arts, as illustrated by the creative strategies of the prophets. For a general strategy of pre-evangelism, I will briefly describe one developed by Francis Schaeffer for his own ministry to young and alienated people in Western culture, and which he used in developing L'Abri fellowship.[47]

V. THE STRATEGY OF PRE-EVANGELISM

Suppose for the sake of argument that Christianity is true and that a worldview or plausibility structure is defined by the beliefs it requires someone to hold to be a member in good standing of the group or culture that holds it. Then even when an unbeliever holds a plausibility structure that is antithetical to the claims of God and Christ at the points where it distinguishes itself from Christianity, their nature remains created in God's image and a constant witness to God's truth, which the unbeliever must work at keeping suppressed, as we discussed in the previous chapter. We may suppose then that there is a kind of cognitive dissonance between the non-believers perspective and other beliefs held by the non-believer that are formed in his or her experience of the real world. But if we push the non-believer's beliefs to the limits of their logical implications, their consequences become increasingly difficult to reconcile with their other beliefs. Thus the non-believer must decide again and again how far they are willing to go to maintain their unbelief. By pushing the non-believer to work out the consistency of their

---

[47] Francis A. Schaeffer, *The God Who is There*, IVP Books; 30th Anniversary Edition, 1998.

plausibility structure, we force the choice between denying Christ and denying reality, if Christianity is true.

Because of the fall, non-believers are primarily disposed to deny God and explain the universe without Him. But because of common grace - the universal grace of God to all that keeps people from being as sinful as they can be for the sake of humanity and the mission of the Church - no one lives in complete consistency with their anti-Theistic point of view. So the gospel leads us to expect to find points of tension between a person's non-Christian beliefs and the remaining beliefs that keep him or her from being logically pushed off the face of reality.

So the strategy is for the Christian to step into a relationship with the non-Christian, say, as a fellow employee or a family member, and then to explore their view, when circumstances are appropriate for doing so, and find such points of tension in their thought and way of living. Having found such, we invite non-believers to work out the implications of their views until they see that those implications include denying what remains important and precious to them. They thus have to decide which they want to keep. Consistency will not let them keep both.

This is particularly an issue with modernism, since if modernism is true then we are nothing but matter in motion plus time and chance. There is no basis for meaning in life as we saw when we looked at the issue of meaning in Chapter 6. In that chapter, we argued that the only stable views were nihilism and theism. So in so far as a view departs from theism, the logic of its beliefs reduces the view to nihilism. But it is not really possible for a person to act consistently with a nihilistic background as we saw. We also saw that a conspicuous belief in nihilism has an acidic impact on behavior to the detriment of the virtues that sustain the disciplined pursuits of society. In both senses, nihilism is unlivable.

Consequently, the modernist is in one or more ways in tension with life. Such tensions may be in the form of straight up inconsistencies of belief, or they may be in the form of discrepancies between faith and practice, or they may be in the form of overwrought compartmentalization between areas of understanding or life. Often when we discover them we find that they are insulated by some set of ad hoc suppositions which only are there to provide cover for the tension they are hiding. We should expose them when we find them for what they are.

For example, I was talking to a graduate student in history who was not a believer. He was lamenting the lack of scientific rigor in the methodology of history and was thinking of changing his program to study psychological behaviorism - the view that all the phenomena of human behavior can be explained by conditioning, like in training a dog to respond to your voice. Such a view would certainly fit with the belief in scientific naturalism.

We went on to discuss the few existing graduate programs that did this kind of research and the general difficulties in changing grad programs. Then I suggested that even if he could not get into such a program, he could still pursue this kind of research project in a history department by doing a historical study into the events conditioning the behavior of historians that determine how they write history. At this, he got sour and said that such a project would amount to historicism, the belief that what counted as "history" was relative to the historian and their conditions rather than the facts, and that would undermine history as a kind of inquiry.

I replied that he could not be a behaviorist and deny the legitimacy of that kind of project. Either deny the possibility of historical enquiry or give up the view that humans are nothing but the sum of their conditioning. He gave me quite a look. This illustrates a point of tension in his thinking. The consistent thing to do would be to allow this kind of research and embrace historicism. However, as he clearly saw at that point, this illustrates the self-defeating character of naturalism and undermines the pursuit of even truths of science. There must be more than nature alone if doing social science is paradigmatically plausible.

Of course, we should be prepared to receive blows as well as give them. We should examine ourselves for our own inconsistencies at being Christians and deal with them. And we should admit our own failures. We should also be prepared to deal with objections against our view. If such a process is successful, our non-believer will be profoundly unhappy. We need to be careful to be sensitive to our friend so he or she is not tempted to extreme behavior, like suicide.

How dare we do this? Only because we think that the Gospel is true. It is right to provoke this awakened sense of need that we address with the gospel. When we do, we must make clear that by the gospel we intend the truth and are not merely the offering of a pragmatic palliative. The greater cruelty would be to allow humans to die in judgment and despair.

VI. CHRISTIAN TACTICS

When I started out trying to reason with non-Christians, I used to always try to find the "kill shot" - the one thing I could say that would blow up the whole argument of my opponent. What I have come to appreciate more and more is the "nudge". Rather, than always going for the throat, it preserves your contact with a person simply to make a little point here and a little point there and let the cumulative effect of your comments take its toll over time. Very often one can make points without making assertions. It is always good to cultivate a sense for good questions and for allowing implications to speak for themselves. Often asking the right question invites the non-Christian to make the point rather than you.

We should challenge ourselves to use our imagination and creativity. C. S. Lewis said that he was converted in his imagination before he was converted in his reason. We tend not to think of creativity as playing a role in communication. Remember that we need to address the non-believers' plausibility structure and this can be done by inviting them to explore another world in writing or art with a different point of view. You may not be an artist but there are often ordinary pastimes and hobbies where people are invited to try being creative no matter how talented.

Finally, we must continue even in the mode of defending the faith, to show palpable love and affirmation. Love for one another is the true mark of the Christian. "By this shall all men know that you are my disciples, that you love one another." Two vital features of a church that is attractive to non-believers and

119

that the congregation is not afraid to face tough questions and that they show genuine love for one another. The Gospel is about communication, but communication is not just in words. We have to be and do as well as say the gospel. Discipleship is not just a transfer of information but also an imaging of the character of Christ.

In part 1, we focused on objections to Christian faith to help believers confronted in college or other secular institutions with questions about their faith to be confident that there were answers to many hard questions, to be discerning about how institutions select a dominant plausibility structure other than evidence and argument, and to see that Christianity is a comprehensive worldview that gives structure and purpose to everything we do. If Christianity is properly understood, it would be hard to imagine anything more motivating and exciting than being a Christian.

Part II

Making a Case for the Christian Faith

8. "I Would Sooner Defend a Mountain Lion!"

Charles Haddon Spurgeon, the great English Baptist Preacher of the 19th Century, once was asked about the defense of the Scriptures. He replied, "Defend the Bible? I would sooner defend a mountain lion!" His attitude reflects the great sufficiency of the Scriptures in defending themselves and that the basis of Christian belief is self-authenticating. Some, however, take this to mean that there is no place and therefore no duty for the Christian to give a defense of the Christian Faith. As we will see, this is not the case.

I. INTRODUCTION: FRANCOIS' STORY

We begin by telling a story about Francois (not his real name). Fran was a graduate student ahead of me in my university's philosophy program and a staunch Catholic. He had come from a college in his home province in Canada, where he studied philosophy. In that school's department, there were Christians who were professors but most of the department were not friendly to Christian faith and were quite outspoken with their criticisms. However, from Fran's point of view, it seemed that the Christian professors said nothing in response to any of these objections. From this, Fran had concluded that they were silent because they had nothing worth saying, and so further concluded that there really was no reasonable justification for Christianity. It must be nonsense as the hostile professors said. At that point he became an atheist.

However, when he finished his degree and went to our school for doctoral studies, he found that there were also Christian professors and professors unfriendly to Christianity. However, there was a difference. The Christian professors at this school did have things to say in response to criticisms, things that were all up to the measure of their evident stature as accomplished and articulate philosophers who had earned the respect of their adversarial colleagues for their work in the field. Fran realized that there was indeed much to say in favor of theism, that there were even opening frontiers of rewarding research into what we may assess by reason that supports theism. He then realized that it wasn't that his previous professors lacked reasons for believing, but that they had lacked the courage to express them. Fran then reclaimed his faith and became a worthy philosophical defender of it.

II. APOLOGETICS: NEGATIVE & POSITIVE

Francois' story illustrates the need and importance for being able to give reasons for belief in Christ, what we call the discipline of APOLOGETICS. The word "apology" often refers to an expression of conviction and regret wrongdoing against another person, used to seek forgiveness and reconciliation with the offended party. But the original setting of the word is in the context of the courtroom and refers to the defendant's defense of his conduct, showing that he was not guilty of what he is being charged. (The word itself comes from APO (back) and LOGOS (word) – "to give a word back (in reply), to defend".) But what is "apologetics" as a discipline?

We have grown accustomed to thinking of apologetics as a branch of ministry, as a part of Christian education, preaching, missions, and/or evangelism. For example, Francis Schaeffer defines apologetics as "the defense and communication of the gospel". While this captures a genuine and proper truth with respect to the use of apologetics, it tends to obscure the motive and purpose of apologetics in a way that makes the task of apologetics harder by focusing only on the personal value of apologetics. But the aim of apologetics is to defend the possibility of theology as a science, where "science" is understood in the broad sense of being an objective inquiry into some existing objects by means that allow for the disclosure of their nature to the mind, in short a disciplined inquiry into the truth. Biology as a science, for example, requires biological realities to be understood, a mind to understand biological realities such as naturally living microbes, animals, and plants, and methods and means so that the biologist is able to discover the operations of biological objects.

Similarly then, theology as a science in this sense has its Object, God and His relation to His Creation, the theologian as *homo pietas* as the inquiring subject to receive knowledge of God, and Revelation as that means by which God makes Himself known to man. Apologetics then defends the principles or sources that make theology as a science possible: God, Religious Man, Revelation, and the additional sources supported by these: Christ, the Church, and the Scriptures. To compare apologetics to systematic theology, both study and defend the whole of Christianity, but systematic theology studies and defends the full form and essence of Christianity in its particular affirmations while apologetics studies and defends Christianity in its sources. Systematic theology studies the fully grown tree; apologetics establishes the seeds the tree came from. So before we can talk of how best to incorporate apologetic arguments into our teaching and ministry, we first and foremost must establish that theology is the knowledge of God and that Christianity is the truth.[48]

Of course, defending a claim also involves replying to reasonable objections to it, such as the problem of evil and suffering and evidence for evolution. In Part I, we focused on some common objections to the claim that Christianity is true. As we will see in this chapter, the Christian is already in possession of reasons for the truth of Christianity, even if not fully aware of the fact, but enough aware to have a settled peace of mind about it. For that reason, dealing with objections can seem more urgent since one would have continued to believe if they hadn't encountered the objection. Answering objections can thus be a factor that contributes to the hygiene of personal faith, and is a very valuable discipline. But personal faith is not able to confront critics who believes they have personal reasons for holding beliefs contradictory to the Christian Faith. For that, something must be said by way of making the case for Christiani-

---

[48] B. B. Warfield, *Apologetics*, *"The* New Schaff-Herzog Encyclopedia of Religious Knowledge,"* edited by Samuel Macauley Jackson, D.D., LL.D., vol. i, pp. 232-238, copyright by Funk and Wagnalls Company, New York, 1908.

ty to show that the opponent's views are still not true. Francois illustrates that the apparent lack of a case can be difficult for one's faith. On the other hand, if one has a positive case for Christianity, that is a reason for rejecting many proposed objections to Christianity. We call the replies given to proposed objections to Christianity NEGATIVE APOLOGETICS and reasons given in behalf of affirming Christianity POSITIVE APOLOGETICS.

III. FAITH & REASON

A person may say "I know that there are still some cookies left in the jar". Another might look and discover that the jar is empty and then say "You didn't really know it. You only believed it." Belief and knowledge, though often set as rivals, are very closely tied together. On a standard analysis of knowledge, if I know a proposition, it must at least be true, something that I believe, and something that I am justified or warranted to believe, so that truth, belief, and reason (in one or another of its senses) are necessary for knowledge. But further, even though we can speak and think of belief as distinct from knowledge or reason in the abstract, psychologically belief formation is not separable from coming to know something and coming to think of something as true. Belief is in order to know. And so, belief is in itself a compelled assent. One believes something to be true when one believes he has sufficient evidence for accepting it as true. So the psychology of belief formation and of coming to know fails to provide a basis for distinguishing between faith and reason. However, it still seems there are natural ways the two should be distinguished.[49]

Some try to make an exclusive dichotomy between the two, while others try to explain one in terms of the other. But it seems that the two can be both distinguished and related in the following ways. In terms of the objects of reason and belief, they seem to be overlapping sets. There are things we only know through reason, such as the laws of science, and things that we only know through faith, such as that Jesus died for our sins, but also things we know through either one, such as that the world depends on God for its existence. We certainly cannot reject the last one based on a claim that reason must be separate from faith.

But in terms of reason and faith as means, it seems that we distinguish reason as referring to means of direct acquaintance, whether by the senses or by immediate intellectual insight, and faith as referring to means of indirect acquaintance such as believing based on credible testimony. However, it's clear that these means operate in an interactive way. Testimony cannot be accepted unless the recipient is able to judge that it is worthy of credit through reason. On the other hand, to accept something as true on the basis that it is judged to be credible is a matter of faith. The fruitfulness of results that comes from allowing the interaction of both faith and reason draws them forward as a fecund circle. It was Augustine who became well known for attempting to articulate this dynamic and necessary interaction after his

---

[49] B. B. Warfield, "Faith in its Psychological Aspects", *The Princeton Theological Review*, ix. 1911, pp. 537 - 566.

frustration with those who boasted that they were following reason alone. Instead standing on reason alone and proving the faith exclusively from that, we proceed from faith in order to seek understanding.

IV. KNOWING & SHOWING

In order to address some of the concerns some Christians may have about the use of reason in apologetics, I want to make a distinction between knowing that something is true and showing that something is true. Some of the ancient Greeks held that if you cannot prove your claims to be true, then you do not know they are true. They may be true and you may believe they are true, but such true opinions are more miracle than knowledge. However, imagine that you are out for a stroll by the lake in the evening, something you don't usually do, and there is no one else around. The next day you are charged with a murder that took place in your office at the time you were walking. The weapon was a knife taken from your kitchen, which has no one else's prints on it but yours.

All the evidence points to you and no one can confirm your alibi. The jury convicts you and you are sentenced for life. Does the jury's conviction mean you have to believe you really did the murder after all? Does it dismiss your personal recollection of being by the lake? Of course not. So we see that the fact that you are not able to prove something does not mean you do not know it. According to the Apostle Paul in Romans 1, there is knowledge of God that is immediately discerned in the things that God has made, showing both His power and divinity, that people receive but suppress in unrighteousness. This could be true of all people, even those of humble means who would know that God exists but could not show it.

Pascal was a Christian who wrote about what he called "reasons of the heart of which reason knows nothing".[50] At first, this sounds to us as if he is talking of something non-rational such as the emotions. But in the context, it is clear that what he means are self-evident intrinsically true propositions such as "A whole is greater than any of its parts" or "Nothing can be red all over and green all over at the same time". Of course these are inherently rational, but in Pascal's day, "rationality" had become reserved for the scientific procedures and methods of reasoning - the reason which knows nothing of reasons of the heart. There is a distinction to be made between reasoning, which refers to the practices of inquiry and deduction, and reason which refers to the receptive power of the mind to recognize self-evident truths and necessary connections, things we can know to be true whether we can show this or not. For now, I want to accept both reason and reasoning, even though the former has become controverted. (However, if something is controverted, it does not follow that it really is controversial.)

Many substantial propositions are of this sort such as that if nothing exists, then nothing is possible and that if something is possible there have to be at least things that exist to sufficiently explain that possibility and that whatever begins to exist must have a cause and so on. We must also admit that there are some

---

[50] Blaise Pascal, *Pensees*, 1669.

sense based propositions which are certainly true such as "This is a coffee cup." But even a list of all the self-evident truths, incorrigible truths, certainties of perception, and truths by definition would not necessarily exhaust all the things we could immediately know. To claim the contradictory would be self-defeating, since such a claim would be asserted as necessarily true but yet not fall under any of those categories.

It is conceivable, and from the point of view of faith is taken as true, that the mind is equipped with a natural facility to reliably recognize God in nature and in oneself, something John Calvin described as man's sense of Deity, both in believers and unbelievers. While it is true that someone could say that "I have an immediate belief that Wotan exists" or "I have an immediate belief that the universe is random and chaotic and without a divine presence", this would make no difference to the Christian for the question of their knowing that God exists. Just as there is a sense of Deity in creation, there is also one in the Holy Scripture so that both God and the Gospel are attested and the whole Christian faith can be known. This shows that the believer can be in a position to know that Christianity is true and that there is nothing that could make it to be false.[51]

However, the confrontation with the person who claims to have immediate knowledge that an anti-Christian view is true illustrates the need to be able to show the truth and to give a reason for one's beliefs. We need to see how far we can go in

---

[51] Plantinga, A. & Wolterstorff, N., eds. *Faith and Rationality: Reason and Belief in God*. Notre Dame: University of Notre Dame Press, 1983.

making our beliefs clear and the reasons for holding them explicit. Human reasoning may not quite capture the evidence in proportion to the certainty that we are able to have in the way that we know the truth. We need to try to show that our arguments make it easier to believe in Christianity than not to do so. For that, we will use a variety of evidences. Some will be philosophical arguments that aim to be demonstrations and proofs. We will also use scientific and historical arguments that try to show that the Christian view is the most likely to be true given the facts.

Finally, we will use arguments to show that, even if the state of the evidence is indeterminate to show the truth of the Christian claim, it is still more reasonable to believe the claim than otherwise. Over all, we want to aim for the same type of conviction possible to a courtroom considering the evidence in a case, or to a person who is trying to decide when it is safe to cross a busy street. Even though the presentation of such evidence falls short of mathematical certainty, it could provide enough for a moral certainty sufficient to oblige the faith of the audience. That does not mean that we necessarily expect the evidence to actually move the audience.[52]

Someone may object that we are thus putting Christianity on a weak foundation of human reason. There is no guarantee that our arguments are never going to be confronted with arguments even more clever later on. Why should we make faith depend on awful fortunes of arguments which have gone back

---

[52] C. Stephan Evans, *Why Believe?: Reason and Mystery as Pointers to God*, William B. Eerdmans Publishing Company; Revised edition, 1996.

and forth over history? The answer is that accepting the truth of Christianity is not founded on our arguments but rather the arguments are signs and pointers to the truth. The idea is to point the non-believer to the objective grounds for belief. Our case is not based on the feeble telescope but on Jupiter to which it points.

Another person might say that our use of arguments is disingenuous since we are using Christianity to decide what to defend and then picking out the arguments that look like they are defending Christianity. How does that show that theology is a science rather than an ideology? Let us grant for the sake of argument that the person making the objection is right. It still is required that such arguments be good arguments that stand on their merits apart from their role in supporting Christianity. Thus they still make contributions to theology as a science. The "Answers in the back of the textbook" objection is a kind of ad hominem fallacy. However, as we said in Chapter 7, the vulnerability of our arguments to criticism illustrates a sense in which Christianity is open to falsification in that something can come up that forces us to abandon or alter our case for Christianity, such as what happened with Galileo or with the discovery of natural selection in the 19th century. And we can hypothesize other kinds of falsification such as finding the body of Jesus. The first created real difficulties but the case for Christianity adapted to them with ultimate loss – which is what we are to expect if Christianity is true. The second though would be a case that could only be hypothetical but not really possible if Christianity is true.

V. EVIDENCE, RESPONSIBILITY, AND THE ROLE OF THE SPIRIT

As we said, evidence compels belief, but this kind of compulsion is compatible with being responsible for our beliefs. We may resist following the evidence as far as it goes or we may obscure or hide ourselves from the evidence. We may employ all kinds of informal fallacies of reasoning or may subscribe to false assumptions which alter our estimation of the evidence. Consequently, some think that since Christians say that every person was radically affected by Adam's fall into sin such that no one can change their own stubborn heart to receive and welcome God, there is no point in trying to argue with them. Better to just preach the Gospel to them and trust the Holy Spirit to crack the nut.

Some however fail to understand the doctrine of humanity's depravity in the right way. They understand it to mean exhaustive depravity, that humans are as bad as they can be. This is both unbiblical and false in experience. The Bible makes clear that God has not left himself without a witness in creation, that even sinners know how to take care of their children, and that Government is God's provision for the restraint of sin. By various means of common grace, God restrains the extent of human depravity for the sake of His longsuffering and to allow the gospel message to go forth. What depravity means instead is radical depravity, that every area of a person's life has been affected by sin such that nothing they do is unalloyed and sufficient for moral credit. Consequently, much real good can be and is done by sinners not in the faith including in the areas of thought and inquiry.

Another way to see this is in the doctrine of the image of God in Man. This is often spoken of in a wider and a narrower sense. In the wide sense all men are made and still bear the image of God as his creatures. They have a nature that reflects the Nature and Power of their author, which is what makes them human. On the other hand, only few bear the image of God in the sense that they reflect God's character as well as His nature and even then only by a degree of perfection due to sanctifying grace. However, some confuse the loss of the image of God in the latter sense with the former sense, as if to say that man in essence is something else other than what God created him to be. Since this former sense includes man as a rational agent, it is as much to say that man has become essentially irrational. But then men cannot be held responsible for not knowing God in any sense since he could not know God in such a condition. But we affirm that it is all humans being made in God's image in the broader sense that gives us the basis for a natural point of contact for apologetics. The position that says man is exhaustively depraved and that-God's image is totally lost we reject as a kind of Hyper-Calvinism.[53]

But we as Christians do think that man is depraved and that he suppresses the truth in unrighteousness. Cognitively, this involves all kinds of bad forms of reasoning but in particular it

---

[53] Michael Sudduth, *The Reformed Objection to Natural Theology (Ashgate Philosophy of Religion Series)*, Ashgate, 2009.

involves tacitly accepting false assumptions as having a kind of status similar to the reasons of the heart mentioned earlier. This is important because it determines what the thinker accepts as probable or plausible, as we saw in Chapter 1. Even though depravity is in every individual's heart, such false assumptions are often acquired through participation in society or by picking up certain habits of inquiry. Examples of such assumptions include things like:

i. Smart people are skeptical, so doubt is good.
ii. University professors are atheists because they know more.
iii. Science is the only reliable way to know things.
iv. Religion cannot be public because it only has private reasons.
v. Enlightened people are tolerant and undogmatic.

We not only then must examine evidence and arguments for belief but if belief, is still not compelling we need to ask if there are any false assumptions that are affecting our plausibility structure and disinclining us to accept the truth. Our entertainment of these assumptions is a matter of our responsibility so that no excuse can be made for having them. To deal with such assumptions, we must recognize them, make them explicit, identify their source (the media, college, the street) to see whether the source is not necessarily reliable or may be subject to institutional forces that prevent from being objective, and show that they are not necessarily true.[54]

[54] J. P. Moreland, *Love God with All Your Mind: The Role of Reason in the Life of the Soul*, NavPress, 1997.

In dealing with humanity's responsibility and recognizing a moral dimension to reasoning and believing, we also acknowledge the role of the Holy Spirit. The Bible tells that it is the Holy Spirit in particular that assures the Christian of the truth of her faith and of her membership in the body of Christ. (Romans 8) This is often described as the testimony of the Holy Spirit. However, this testimony is not a direct speaking of the Spirit to the believer but is rather recognized as a necessary ministry in recovering the believer's ability to recognize the truth of the Gospel and see the basis of her security clearly. Since the Christian knows that she would otherwise, as enslaved to sin, never have acknowledged nor continued to acknowledge the evidence that supports the truth of Christianity except for the work of the Spirit, she thus recognize the Spirit's active Presence in her life enabling her to focus on the evidence and judge it rightly. And this implies the further fact that the Holy Spirit Himself is assuring her of the truth. This is the testimony of the Spirit.[55]

However, John 17 tells us that the Spirit (the Counselor) has come into the world to convict it of sin, of righteousness, and of judgment. Specifically, there is a truth guiding ministry of the Holy Spirit that is given to non-Christians also which provides for the preparation and spread of the gospel. We see then, that the Holy Spirit works mediately through the preaching of the gospel, but also immediately on the minds and hearts of unbelievers keeping them from escaping the claims of Christ and from totally suppressing the truth. It is this work of the Holy Spirit which also

---

[55] Herman Bavinck, *The Certainty of Faith*, Paideia Press, 1980.

serves as a point of contact with the unbeliever. In fact this doctrine gives us confidence to do apologetics, understanding that the work involved only has hope of persuading because of the sovereignty of the Spirit. Therefore, we should make our apologetic offerings in absolute dependence on the Spirit in all humility and submission.

VI. CONCLUSION: BE PREPARED TO GIVE A DEFENSE

Given these considerations, we shouldn't be surprised to find so many examples in the Scriptures of prophets (Isaiah) and apostles (Peter at Pentecost, Paul in Athens, Luke's books, Paul's letters) using reasons and arguments to persuade their recipients to be led by reason to Christ. We should not be surprised at the extensive use of evidence and logic by Jesus (John 9) in his earthly ministry. Finally, we should not be surprised that we are exhorted by Peter to be prepared to give a defense for the Reason for the Hope within us (1 Peter 3.15). The final argument for positive apologetics is that by example and by apostolic dictate, Christ commands us to do it.

9. Science and Skepticism

Let's begin this chapter with a puzzle. See if you can solve it before reading the next paragraph. You have a bathroom that is tiled with uniformly square tiles in a specific shade of blue that you really like. However, one day you notice that one of the tiles has fallen out and smashed on the floor. You are resolved to find a replacement tile that is the same exact shade of blue as the others. Unfortunately, after searching all over town you find only one place that sells tiles in that color. Further, the only tiles they have in that color are square but have exactly half the surface area of the tile you are replacing. You resign yourself to the idea that you are going to have to buy and cut these smaller tiles to fill the space and keep the same color. *What is the smallest number of tiles you need to buy and what is the fewest number of cuts you will have to make?*

There are two possible solutions to this puzzle. Both answers require two tiles and two cuts. One way is to cut each tile in half along the diagonal of the square. The other is to leave one square alone but make two cuts along both diagonals of the other square. Either way, the pieces can be arranged to exactly fit and fill the space. Both solutions involve the same principle, namely that a square whose side is the diagonal of another square is always twice the area of that other square, a specific type of instance of the Pythagorean Theorem: The sum of the square of the hypotenuse of a right triangle is equal to the sum of the squares of the other two sides.

But the point of the example is, if you solved this for yourself, that without even actually having a real bathroom, you not only know that this would solve the problem, but you even know that you know this. You may have come to a point where it seemed impossible to solve and where you did not know what to try next, a point where you realized you did not know the answer. Yet, it turned out that you were not stuck for long and now you know the answer. Furthermore, your knowledge cannot be based on an accumulation of evidence since this would be a generalization from one imaginary instance, not a generalization from many experimental instances. In this case, the mind is a box out of which we get more than we put in. How is that possible?[56]

I. TWO ATTITUDES TOWARD PHILOSOPHY

The late, distinguished philosopher Robert Nozick in an interview had some words for philosophers he called Thought Police, namely philosophers who had a certain way they thought philosophy should be done and certain conclusions that philosophy ought to hold – a kind philosophical ideology. To Nozick, philosophy should not be so hidebound but engage in the free play of conceptual gambling and expect to find surprising and counter-intuitive results. Such philosophical "mucking around" should be encouraged. It develops philosophical potential and

---

[56] This puzzle is based on Plato's dialogue, the Meno.

has yielded great insights. We would not be where we are today without it.

However, Stuart Hackett, a Christian philosopher, had other ambitions for philosophy. For him, philosophy ought to be reflection on the intellectual aspect of one's personal value system or worldview, the life-long effort to systematically clarify, coherently interpret, and critically evaluate our otherwise jumbled and vaguely perceived core commitments, moving more and more towards a worldview that makes sense of the world and effectively guides one's life. While not saying that everyone has a religious commitment, he does suggest that everyone has, whether they face the fact or not, a philosophy of life and its ultimate concerns. Their only choice is to have a conscientiously developed one or a haphazard one.[57]

Obviously, there is no logical incompatibility between having these attitudes which seem good taken by themselves. It may be that neither one is always the most appropriate attitude to take in every situation but that there are situations where one or the other takes appropriate priority. At any rate, our embracing and cultivating the attitude recommended by Hackett should not be construed as a rejection of the attitude encouraged by Nozick.

Following Nozick, there is no need to worry about the ultimate conclusions or absolute background of our philosophical reflections. But in examining our life, there is the important question of truth and value. *Is it possible that we are able to fathom anything about any great features of the world?* Hack-

---

[57] Stuart C. Hackett, 1984.

ett's project must assume the answer is yes in order to be sufficiently motivated and to justify the cost of those things we are giving up to pursue it. This is the view we want to defend in this book.

Our purpose in the next two chapters is to address the problem of knowledge in the modern worldview and to defend the possibility of a serious "science" of God. As we saw in Chapter 1, the heretical imperative implies skepticism of any knowledge outside of science. Therefore, moral and religious perspectives are encouraged to be radically diversified and replaced over time, since they cannot claim to be based in fact, but the deliverances of science are to be treated as sacrosanct. But in this chapter, we want to show how in history, these modern commitments have led to skepticism about science. In the next chapter we will argue against skepticism.

II. A CONVERSATION WITH MODERNITY

As we saw in various ways in the first part of the book, the plausibility structure of our society, especially applied to science and religion, makes it very difficult to affirm truth. What truths we may hold are those vouchsafed to us by the natural sciences, while any claim to any other domain of truth not only may be suspended but ought to be rejected. When it comes to matters of value, our business is not to reasonably limit explanations but multiply them beyond any rational utility through a surplus of perspectives. There is nothing we can settle about self, others, morality, or religion. How did we get to this point?

It is practical to start with Rene Descartes. Before his time, in the Middle Ages, the theologians had inherited from the Greeks, particularly Plato and Aristotle, a metaphysical view which secured the possibility of knowledge and philosophical inquiry. However, in the later Middle Ages and the rise of the Renaissance, thinkers were led to the rediscovery of skepticism and the skeptical ancient Greek authors. Further, the conflicts between the monastic Orders, the Reformation and the Catholic Magisterium, and the Aristotelians and the new science, led to a general loss of confidence in church authority and new confidence in inductive science. Where the theologians came to be seen as always disagreeing, the new scientists seemed to have the resources to settle disagreements. The new possibilities opened by a focused concentration on science were worth pushing aside the old establishments including theology and Scholastic philosophy. An alternative picture of nature, corpuscularianism – the view that everything is composed of little extended bits of material mechanically bouncing off each other - had become the paradigm view of nature because it motivated these newer projects. Skepticism was to have a fine revenge on scholasticism.

Descartes stands on the bridge between the medieval period and the early modern period of thought. In his brief work *Meditations on the First Philosophy*, he makes the shift from starting with the presumption of possibility of inquiry – the view that all knowledge begins with wonder - to starting with a methodical approach to doubt. We normally take the world as we see it by assuming that our senses and our ability to reason are reliable. But what if my perception of the world was just a dream that I am having? My experiences would be the same yet they would not be truly about the world. Further, what if I was haunted by an evil demon that always interfered with my thought process? Then it would still seem that 17,136/48 = 357 every time I thought of it, but every time I do the demon steps in, so that while it seems that 17,136/48 = 357 to me, it really equals 159. My experience in thinking would appear to be the same with or without the demon. Descartes then concludes; since for all we know it is possible that these strange hypotheses might be true, and since I have no way of discerning from my experience to know that they are false, then it is illegitimate to suppose they are false. So I cannot be certain of what my reasoning or senses tell me, and thus that all belief I have from sense or reason is no knowledge at all. Since natural science relies ultimately on mathematical reasoning and sense observation, science is also lost.

However, following John Locke, in his *Essay on Human Understanding*, we may question the validity of that conclusion. Descartes is making a demand for absolute certainty in order to have knowledge. But this does not square with what we call knowledge in our ordinary experience. We claim to know even if the grounds are only probable. If I asked you if you know where your car is, I expect you would say you did even though you admit in the abstract that someone might have stolen your car since you saw it last. This could only mean that for you probable evidence is sufficient to call your belief knowledge. If so, we do not need to rule out skeptical hypotheses to legitimately say we know.

Locke grants that we cannot compare the contents of our mind to the world apart from the mind to see if there is correspondence between them. Yet there is a sense in which we test to confirm if reasoning and senses are reliable simply by relying on them, just as we can test to see if a bridge is safe by trying to cross it. Though a successful track record is no proof of reliability, it is sufficient when we have no other source of confirmation and when we think the goal is worth the risk, which is the case here. Granting the reliability reason and the senses, we can add that while Descartes' skeptical hypotheses are consistent, they are not especially likely. Our normal assumptions provide a more economic explanation than his since his presupposes an appearance that would be the case if our faculties were reliable and then adds a feature which twists them to a get a skewed result.

On the other hand, Locke's own starting point creates problems. Where Descartes is looking for absolutely certain reasons that transcend these doubt-causing hypotheses, Locke wants to say that all of our knowledge is based on experience alone, that there is nothing in the mind that is not first in the senses. He calls the mind a "blank slate", totally clean until the pen of our senses writes its marks on the page. This analysis would also apply to even abstract ideas and mathematical truths, such as $17,136/48 = 357$. It would not be by immediately seeing that $17,136/48 = 357$ is true that we think that it is true, but rather by having repeated and reinforced experiences of the numerical terms of such an equation being together and forming a strong habit of association in our mind.

This view is much more rigorously stated by David Hume, in his *Enquiry Concerning Human Understanding*, by his claim that the contents of our mind are nothing else except those vivid impressions from the senses that we have at the moment and the faded reflections or "ideas" those impressions leave in the mind. If that is all there is, the only thing our judgments can be are either those that are confirmed or confirmable by immediate experience or those in which old ideas are bound and reinforced together by habits of mental association. Thus, if Locke's "blank slate" doctrine is true, then skepticism about most things is unavoidable, such as moral obligations (which are neither trivial associations nor visible to the eye), universals, spiritual beings, or God.

But Hume also showed that if Locke was right about the mind being a blank slate, we are also not able to know that little bits of matter move by being bumped into by other bits of matter. All we see is one bit stopping right where another bit starts moving, with no impressions of a "transfer of energy" going on, so we have no impression and no idea of being "caused". Similarly, scientific theories are supposed to be generalizations of natural behavior that are characterized as laws of nature. However that assumes we can count on nature to behave uniformly throughout space and time. Since we cannot have a possible impression of the whole of space and time, we cannot make generalizations about laws. So science, which explains by providing mechanical explanations according to natural laws, is also impossible if Locke and Hume are right about the mind being a "blank slate".

But as Immanuel Kant pointed out, in reply to Hume in his *Critique of Pure Reason*, there are many things that we know to be true that we could not have learned just by either impressions or the associations of ideas. For example, we know that a square constructed on a diagonal of a given square will be twice its area, without acquiring it through habit, as the puzzle that begins this chapter shows. When we see what the answer is, *we also see that we see that it is the answer* even if that is the one time we encountered such a problem. Also, Isaac Newton knew that the laws of inertia and momentum held throughout the physical universe, even in space beyond where he could see. Newton's laws could not have been just a generalization or a habitual connection of ideas. So there must be more in the mind beside ideas and impressions that made such knowledge possible. Impressions may provide the occasion for such beliefs but they are not adequate to explain them. As another philosopher, Gottfried Leibniz, said in reply to Locke's "blank slate" doctrine, "There is nothing in the mind except what is first in the senses – except the mind."

So an adequate account that makes science possible is going to have to include a reliable reception of knowledge from experience but also a pre-existing power in the mind that knows apart from experience. It is logically possible that some knowledge is already in the mind while some other knowledge is available through experience. In fact, reasoning seems to require both working together. Logic and conceptual relations alone do not commit us to very much about the world outside the mind, but experiences alone would not allow us to predict what might be true beyond them. Science is possible only if we can rely on our innate conceptual powers and our natural belief-forming processes of reasoning and sense perception. However, science cannot prove that these are reliable since their reliability is presupposed by science.

III. THE CHRISTIAN RATIONALIST ALTERNATIVE

Suppose, however, that God does exist. Even without trying to prove that God exists we can conceive of God as the principle cause of both the world and everything in it, as well as of us and our capacity to think. If so, it is conceivable that God could have so created our minds such that they fit with the structure and function of the world. It could thus be that an original creative Mind is the common source of both finite minds and an intelligible world. Just as a computer designer is capable of designing a PC and a printer such that one is able to communicate with the other, God has so designed mankind such that we are capable of understanding the world and each other.

This is similar to the ancient Greek philosopher Plato's answer to the possibility of knowledge. In his dialogue, *Meno*, Plato has Socrates converse with a wealthy man from Thessaly who asks him if virtue can be taught. Socrates tells him that he could not say, not even knowing what virtue is in the first place. This surprises Meno who thinks that he certainly does know what virtue is. But after several attempts by Meno to try to explain the meaning of virtue, Socrates remains unconvinced. This is because Meno's exposition simply gives examples of virtues rather than saying what it is about his examples that makes them all virtues. He has failed to tell Socrates what virtue is and feels totally at a loss to explain it. He realizes that he didn't know what he thought he knew.

Socrates begs him to keep trying but Meno objects. Given Socrates' insistence on knowing the definition of virtue before being able to recognize any examples of it, how could Socrates ever discover what virtue is. The search implies we do not know the answer. Socrates, though, claims that Meno is making a rhetorical argument. If I know what virtue is, I do not need to look for it. And if I do not know what virtue is, I could not find it since I wouldn't even be able to recognize it. Therefore, there is no point for me to look for the meaning of virtue.

Yet perhaps in spite of what Socrates says, this argument does not at first seem so sophistical. To show that it is, Socrates borrows one of Meno's young retainers. Meno assures Socrates that the boy was born in Meno's household and has never learned mathematics anytime during his life. Socrates leads him through a math problem -- how to construct a square twice as large as a given square -- by asking the boy careful questions. At first the boy sounds confident that he can do the problem. But after several suggestions (make the sides twice the length of the original side, make the sides one and a half times the length of the original side), the boy feels as perplexed as Meno did in his quest for a definition for virtue. Instead of complaining, Meno grants that the boy is certainly better off than he was before, because it makes some significant progress to realize that you did not know what you thought you knew. Socrates continues by inviting the boy to construct a new square by using the diagonal (a line that connects one corner to the opposite corner) of the original square as the new square's side. Now the boy sees that this square is exactly twice the size of the original square. The puzzle at the beginning of the chapter is similar to the boy's puzzle - to give you a taste of what he went through.

But the puzzle now is how did he know the answer when it was not explained to him by either Socrates or Meno? He never learned math from Meno and all Socrates did was ask pointed questions. He didn't "teach" the boy in the sense of transmitting any doctrines to him. But if the boy's time with Meno and Socrates is the whole of the boy's life, Socrates says he must have gotten it before then -- before he was born -- and only now recalled it. Thus we have Socrates' thesis that all learning is a kind of recalling something we knew before we were born and forgot at birth. There is a sense in which we already "know" (learned before we were born) and yet another sense in which we do not "know" (have not yet recalled it in this life). Now we see that the argument is sophistical because it trades on an ambiguity. The word "know" does not have the same sense in each occurrence of it in the argument. It is a fallacy of equivocation.

In this example, the doctrine of recollection, along with the associated doctrine of reincarnation, is offered as a hypothesis to explain how the slave boy already knows more than he thinks he knows. It seems that there is something in the mind that was not in the senses, or something the soul knows before the soul experiences anything. Recollection alone is still not enough to explain the things we already know, as Plato spells out in other dialogues such as the *Phaedo* and the *Republic*. If we know something before we were born, then it could not just be in a previous earthly life but in another kind of existence, a place where we saw the truth itself mentally as if by mental sight. Also, in order to see this way, it was necessary that our minds and the truth have a common source, which also provides a kind of intellectual light for the mind to see by. Plato has referred to this Source of being and insight as the "Ultimate Form of the Good".

It is not surprising that Christian thinkers like Augustine saw Plato's "Ultimate Form of the Good" as God Who is the source of all created things and our knowledge of them. Augustine accepted the mystery that Plato presents but explains the connection between things and minds by appealing to creation in the image of God, and to the grace of divine illumination. We are able to know by the light of the "Ultimate Form of the Good". For Plato, that is because we existed from all immortality in an invisible realm where the light of the "Good" illuminated our souls to intellectually see the universal forms before we were ever born into this world. For Augustine, we do not need to have pre-existed since from our creation our minds were able to form the forms of eternal ideas from the mind of God by the light of God illumining our minds to see the ideas in God's own mind.[58]

It is not necessary to totally agree with Plato or Augustine about how knowledge finds its way into the mind apart from experience, but this fact that Socrates finds in the slave boy case

---

[58] Augustine, *Confessions.*

provides a clue that requires some explanation. Does such an explanation require a source beyond natural science?

IV. A CONVERSATION WITH POSTMODERNITY

Kant considers a view like Plato's Good and Augustine's illumination theory, suggesting the thesis that our minds and the world were both created by God to fit with each other, only to reject it for reasons that seem to go back again to Hume. We cannot, he argues, postulate an explanation that claims anything about the world beyond possible experience. Instead, Kant thinks that the most we can say about the conceptual powers we have in the mind is that they structure and shape our experiences to seem to us to make scientific sense. While Kant believes that Hume is wrong about only having experience alone, he does agree with Hume that the infusion of our conceptual powers with our impressions does not tell us anything about the real world. This still preserves science, Kant thinks, because even though science really is not about the world, scientists will agree about how to describe the appearance of world to us because the same conceptual powers are shared by every thinker and lead to the same conclusions. What is "knowledge" and what is "true" is what science will eventually say about experience. You might say that Kant takes the problem raised by Descartes' skeptical hypotheses and gives it back as the answer.

However, how does Kant know that all scientists have the same conceptual powers without being able to step outside the circle of his own conceptually interpreted experiences? My understanding of others is constructed, just as my understanding of the world is constructed. Or how can present thinking tell us about what we will think in the future, since we cannot rule out that our powers may change? Each person, though under the impression of communicating with others, is trapped in the charmed circle of his own conceptually structured experiences. Here the window opens up to suppose that there are many, many, many ways the world might appear, and all we have are perspectives. Kant has planted some of the seeds of post-modern relativism; relativism not just about morals and values, but also about science.

Kant's approach seems self-referentially incoherent. How can one say that everything is just your perspective, and how can you say that there is no way of thinking about what lies outside of your perspective, unless you are thinking about what lies outside of your perspective to distinguish it from your perspective? Also, to claim that all one "knows" is one's own perspective is either a claim about the real world or it is not a claim to be taken seriously. If the former, than it is self-contradictory since one is making a real objective claim. Finally, grant that concepts and perspectives that structure our experience are what we think *with*. That does not imply that concepts and perspective are what we think *of*.

Hume and Kant illustrate the cost of denying that the mind is pre-structured to interpret experience in such a way as to know the truth. Referring back to Chapter 4, they open the door to scientific unrealism, or even scientific irrationalism, but close the door to scientific realism. The modern heretical imperative wants to combine creative relativism about morals and religion with an uncreative and non-relative stance toward science. But if we cannot reason outside of the limits of science, then science itself is relative.

10. Common Sense and the Spirit of Inquiry

In this chapter, we will look at ways a Christian might argue for the possibility of knowledge and a rational approach to Christianity.

I. THE ARGUMENT FROM TRUTH

Plato, Augustine, and Descartes' *Meditations* give different versions of the following argument:[59]

(1) There are some things that I know, and that I know that I know.

(2) If I know some things, then some things are true.

(3) If some things are true, then there must be a correspondence between some thoughts and facts.

(4) If I know some things that are true, then there must be an adequate cause that sees to it that the correspondence between my thoughts and the facts is not accidental but secure.

(5) If there is an adequate cause that sees to it that the correspondence between my thoughts and the facts is not accidental but secure, then God exists.

(6) If God exists, then there could not be any cause in my environment that renders my natural belief forming processes absolutely unreliable.

(7) THEREFORE my belief-forming processes are not absolutely unreliable. Skepticism is rejected and science is possible.

---

[59] Edward John Carnell, *Introduction to Christian Apologetics: A Philosophic Defense of the Trinitarian-Theistic Faith* (The Edward Carnell Library), Wipf & Stock Publishers, 2007.

There are several things that that Augustine and Descartes offer as examples of things that I cannot not know. First is that I cannot not know that I exist. To doubt this is to affirm it since I have to exist in order to doubt that I exist. Hume replies that one cannot have thoughts about oneself that are not also thoughts about oneself in some context of experience or another, such as doubting my existence while drinking a latte at Starbuck's by the college on a sunny afternoon. Since such memories are always associated with thoughts about me, why not say that my "self" is nothing but the set of those individual memories, and not an individual that has them? But Augustine, in *City of God*, points out that his knowledge of his own existence is not something that is necessarily tied to any experience through the senses or through memory. I know me, but I do not experience me. Since his knowledge of his own existence is independent of sensible experience, he is thus certain of that knowledge.

Other things that we cannot not know are the fundamental principles of thought, such as that something cannot both be and not be at the same time in the same sense, and that the whole is always greater than its parts. Once we see what these mean, we see that they must be true. We also know various categories such as substance, causation, and representation by reflecting on ourselves. For example, I know what cause means by stretching out my hand, and I know what representation means when I make my hands into the shape of a bird. Even if I am dreaming or experiencing a hallucination, it does not belie the knowledge of what these mean. Finally, there are paired concepts that I know because to understand one is to understand the other, such as finite/infinite, imperfect/perfect, and contingent/necessary. I might have experiences that illustrate these concepts, but even if these experiences are mirages, they do not fail to illustrate the concepts. So (1) is true.

I cannot know something unless the belief I have of it is true. Truth is just a necessary condition for knowledge, hence (2). By asserting that truth is a necessary condition for knowledge, we mean something is true in a robust way. "Truth" is not merely said of my belief to include it among the thoughts I prefer to take seriously, nor is it simply a name for the fit that my belief has with my other beliefs. These ways of looking at "truth" would amount to just saying that something is "true for me but not necessarily for you". But that is not truth as a necessary condition for knowledge. Truth must mean that what I think is true is true, that the content in my mind represents what is the case. Truth is the correspondence of thought and reality, hence (3).

Truth is necessary for knowledge and correspondence between thought and fact is necessary for truth. Correspondence may be sufficient for truth, but not for knowledge. You could have a brute or "lucky" correspondence. Suppose you accepted a belief based on the flip of a coin. If it lands on heads, then you think that Mr. Smith will be re-elected, but if it lands on tails, he will not. So if it lands on heads, and so you believe that Mr. Smith will get re-elected, and he does get re-elected, then you have a true belief. But you could not say that you *knew* that Mr. Smith would get elected because the relationship between your thought and the truth was by chance. That would still be true if you had a computer with a "random" number generator where each possible number had an event assigned to it, but where the sequence of numbers generated told the exact history of the events. Even though 100% accurate, it would not be true to say that the computer "knows" what events are happening. If scientific naturalism is true, then our situation would be like that computer. Our "knowledge" would just be the brute relation between states and affairs and thoughts, all of which appear as the result of the natural laws operating in a material universe. But then, it would not be knowledge.

Since we do know some things, the relationship between our beliefs and the world must not be accidental or by a blind process, but rather they were brought about intentionally and by design. I could not have seen to it that my thoughts would possibly correspond to the world because I could not see both what my thoughts would be and what the world would be. I can imagine making a printer that communicates with a computer but I cannot imagine how I could have made myself and the world to be possibly corresponding to my thoughts. Yet I know something, so such a thing must be true. So there must be an intelligent and understanding Cause that is responsible and capable of bringing both my mind and the world I know into existence in such a way that they correspond with each other. Further, this Cause must be personal because bringing this relation into being requires intentional purpose, and it must be benevolent being willing to bring this about, hence (4). Such a cause must be an intelligent, personal, benevolent, creative, and the adequate cause of our ideas of Infinity, Perfection, and Necessary Existence. This is what we mean by "God", hence (5).

Finally, if such a God exists, then we have no reason to expect that we are under the control of Descartes' evil demon or that I must be dreaming, because God who is good enough to see to it that I may know some things may keep me from deception. We are even rational in thinking that only a Cause that is an infinitely perfect being could account for my existing with the ideas of infinity and perfection, hence (6). Going back to Descartes' original worry about skepticism arising from an evil demon and his principle that we need a reason to prefer the common sense hypothesis to the evil demon hypothesis, we now have it in the knowledge of a good God. So (7), skepticism about common sense, sense experience, and reasoning, is rejected.

But one might object: we used logic and reasoning just now to work through this argument. As long as we are taking the evil demon story as a serious possibility, we should not be relying on any such process of reasoning. For all we know, the evil demon is making us think we are being led to God, just as the demon leads us to believe falsely that $17136/48 = 357$.

Our answer is similar to one given by Descartes in his fifth meditation. Even though we used a form of argumentation, we were not relying on formal reasoning to establish the conclusion as much as we were using the argument as a roadmap for guiding the mind's attention along the way of the things that we cannot not know to their ultimate source. Once there, one sees immediately, without benefit of the framework of the argument, that God exists and that skepticism is to be rejected. Another way of thinking about this is to say that we have set aside the demon hypothesis for the sake of inquiry. Instead, we have helped ourselves to Locke's rationale for relying on sensation and reason. But now have found even greater cause to rely on it. In distinguishing between the things we know we might not know and the things that we know that we cannot not know, we are also distinguishing between discursive reasoning and reason. The evil demon may affect the former but cannot disturb the latter.

However, the Augustinian view leads to a dilemma. According to Plato the mind is already equipped with all the ideas when it was brought into this world of experience. Experience plays a role in learning, but only by providing occasions to recall these ideas, as a string on your finger reminds you to get something at the store. For example, I say that this marker pen is the same length as that marker pen. But there are many angles from which I can look at both pens and fail to see that they are equal and in fact one may be a micrometer shorter than the other. But I say that their lengths are equal not because of the experience of the pens by itself, but because that experience makes me think of the concept of equality - which in concept is perfectly equal. But this view seems implausible. If the horizon of what I can know is potentially limitless, I must in some sense have an infinite set of ideas already in mind. How might one explain the infinite number of ideas existing in a finite mind? Another problem is how one could have an idea perfectly realized in your mind and then forget it.

On the other hand, an alternative view is that the mind acquires ideas by encountering them embodied as the natural structure of things that makes a thing the kind of thing it is, and abstracting the concept from that natural structure. This explains how our concepts can be true by corresponding with real things– my concepts have the same structure as the natural structure of things. My knowledge that a cat bears live young is made possible because my concept of a cat (which includes the detail that they bear live young) is the same structure as the nature of a cat. Unfortunately, our ability to abstract concepts the same as the natures of things depends on knowing how to identify the relevant features of the thing that count as the nature of it, apart from those features that only happen to be true of it. We could not know which the natural features are unless we already had the concept of the thing. So on the one hand, we could not already have all the concepts, and on the other hand we could not acquire them unless they were already possessed.

Perhaps a possible answer is that at the beginning, we have the potential to acquire concepts, not just Hume's faded ideas but abstract concepts that are intrinsically unified. In this sense the mind is more than what it receives through the senses, yet is still only potentially informed with concepts and not actually possessing them. What is it that informs the mind? Philosopher John Haldane suggests that the mind actualizes its potential to acquire concepts when one learns a language. In learning a language, one learns from being immersed in a world of speakers who already possess the concepts. While we listen and watch our parents and others, they draw our attention to the relevant features of objects which they know because they already understand the concepts. They can show us how to successfully abstract the idea from the object to form our own concepts. From then on, many ideas are formed by reflecting on the concepts acquired.[60]

Consider the case of Helen Keller. Until the day of her breakthrough, she responded to W-A-T-E-R written in her hand as a signal to go get some water as if it was a conditioned response. But her "miracle" came when she finally perceived that W-A-T-E-R is water. Then she discovered the difference between following conditioned responses to signals and possessing symbols that represented kinds of things. Suddenly, she wanted to know what everything else was. It seems that in learning the word for water she stopped just associating the term with that particular liquid, she also acquired the general concept of water.[61]

If this view is true, it avoids the dilemma about concepts since one does not already have all or any concepts at the beginning. One receives help from someone who already has a concept. In the case of those yet to learn a concept, their mind is already potentially able to acquire it. The person teaching them the concept has already acquired it so that her actual concept brings into being the concept for the other person. Yet this shows that this explanation is not complete, since we can ask where the concept teacher acquired her concept from. If we say, from yet another person, the question comes up again. If I introduce an

---

[60] J. C. C. Smart & John Haldane, *Atheism and Theism (Great Debates in Philosophy)*, Wiley-Blackwell; 1st edition, 1996.
[61] Walker Percy, *The Message in the Bottle: How Queer Man is, How Queer Language is, and What One Has to Do with the Other*, Picador; 1st Picador edition, 2000.

infinite sequence of concept teachers who acquired their concepts from other concept teachers, our theory would fail to make sense of knowing. We see that adding one link after another in the chain is not enough to explain a present case of concept acquisition. An infinite series of intermediate concept formers would have the same explanatory inadequacy as a finite series. Therefore, if this theory is correct there must have been a concept teacher that did not need to acquire the concept first. Such a teacher would already have the concept. The simplest explanation would be that there is one First Teacher that originally and always had all the concepts that fit the world, and this we call "*God*". This recalls the picture in Genesis of God conversing with Adam in the Garden. Given our argument from the beginning of this chapter, this fits very nicely.

II. THE ARGUMENT FROM KNOWLEDGE

Our discussion suggests the following argument:

(i)   Either God exists or knowledge is impossible.
(ii) Knowledge is possible.
(iii) Therefore, God exists.

With respect to (ii), it seems that knowledge is possible because some things we not only know but we even know that we know. With respect to (i), positing God would be sufficient to explain knowledge as we have seen in this chapter, and would seem to be necessary according to the previous chapter.

Someone might object to (i) by saying that knowledge can arise from blind processes of nature through regular physical causes, mutations, and adaptation to the environment, so that knowledge is possible without God. The problem with this view is that we think that when someone knows something to be true they do so when their belief is determined by reasons or evidence which compels belief not as a mechanical result but in virtue of their intrinsic and discernible support for the belief. Knowledge requires that beliefs be rationally supported.

Instead, if this naturalistic alternative to (i) is accepted, then beliefs are actually things physically caused. But if I thought the real explanation for my belief was that physical force produced it, I would not have any reason for holding it to be true, unless I had some reason for thinking that the process involved reliably produced true beliefs, but then that would also have to be based on reason or evidence and not just be physically caused. So even if the mechanical process led to a true belief, it would not be knowledge. If my belief that all beliefs are physically caused were itself physically caused, and if the reasons I would give for believing that all belief is physically caused were, as my beliefs, also physically caused, then my belief in them would not be knowledge. Scientific naturalism leads again to skepticism.

Consider the Pythagorean Theorem. To see that this is true is to see that it must always be true. But if my belief now is the result of some mechanical physical process that forces me to believe it, there is no guarantee that the natural laws governing the process will not later this year force me to believe that the Pythagorean Theorem is false as if to say that the theorem was true until 2012 and false afterward. In that case, we would not say that I knew the Pythagorean Theorem.

The total skeptic will deny that (ii) is true by claiming that the knowledge we think we have is only an illusion. But then the skeptic owes an explanation for why it seems that we know something. They may say that what we take to be "knowledge" is just a brute ordering process that brains of the species Homo sapiens impose on experience that makes it "intelligible" even though the result is not really of or about anything in the environment, as we described. Since this "knowledge" is an illusion that persists but does not really interact with anything in the environment, it remains a side effect of evolution that neither helps nor interferes with our environmental fitness for survival and so never gets selected for extinction. In other words, evolution is like the evil demon in Descartes hypothesis. But then, the skeptic's belief that this scenario is possible would by hypothesis also be an illusion.

Also, we can say, with Cardinal Newman, that our own nature as a creature of inquiry that struggles to apply reason to evidence to formulate demonstrations, judge between competing theories, pursue deeper insight and understanding by gathering and sifting facts, by reflection and experiments, in order to come closer and closer to predicting the truth makes us practically certain that we are actually attaining more and more knowledge. We are creatures whose specific tendency is to learn for the sake of learning. This assures us that knowledge is possible in the same way that hunger assures us that food exists and desire for God assures us that God exists, as we discussed in chapter 6. So it seems better to take cases like knowing how to cut the tiles as they appear to be, an instance of genuine knowledge, and to accept that it could only be possible because of divine intelligence.[62]

In this chapter we have argued against skepticism and defended scientific inquiry. But in our argument, we have also argued that knowledge and the possibility of inquiry require God's existence. We have shown that the position that the modern worldview described in Chapter 1 holds, scientific realism with religious unrealism is untenable. By arguing for inquiry, we have also laid the foundation for the possibility of theological inquiry by arguing for existence of God from knowledge. Since God is that cause that makes it possible for one to know, to the extent one knows what he or she knows, he or she also knows something about God.

III. CRITICAL THINKING FOR THOUGHT POLICE

To be perfectly frank, there is no way we can truly cover all the issues that come up in the contemporary discussions of knowledge and skepticism. All we can do at this point is show that the case against truth and knowledge is not necessarily successful and that the sea changes in Western thought did not necessarily dislodge the grounds of the emphasis of earlier

---

[62] John Henry Newman, *An Essay in Aid of a Grammar of Assent*, University of Notre Dame Press; 1st edition, 1992.

periods on wonder rather than doubt. Starting with wonder remains a live option.

What impact does a theistic defense of knowledge have on the pursuit of it? First, there are and must be self-evident principles, such as that a proposition cannot be true and false, the whole is greater than any of its parts, and so on. We claim to know some self-evident truths but not necessarily infallibly. Formulations of what we know that we know are open to revision. In particular, we accept the laws of logic: non-contradiction, identity, excluded middle. In doing so, we do not claim that God must submit to these laws as to a higher authority, but that they are aspects of God's own nature and character as original truth.

Second, we must be willing to commit to the existence of whatever is presupposed by the best explanation of the world. The best explanation will have the greatest balance of relevant great making features (or explanatory virtues) compared to rivals. Great making features include systematic consistency, integral coherence, comprehensive scope, fit with the facts, and practical relevance. We discussed these in chapter 5.

Third, if there remains some doubt that is not muted through demonstration or evidence beyond a reasonable doubt, commitment to the Christian interpretation of life must satisfy the requirements of reasonable risk. This also applies to the choice between skepticism and wonder itself. Some may be content to take in the flow of thought just as it is without raising any questions about it. But others would rather risk seeking the knowledge that may not be available, than miss out on the knowledge that might be.

11. God and the Universe

I. INTRODUCTION: THE TWENTY PLUS WAYS

There are by many reports at least twenty or so arguments for the existence of God that are good, well-formed arguments; from motion or change, from the stability of natural laws, from the specific directedness of natural processes, from information, from consciousness, from knowledge, from the idea of God, from beauty, from universals, from colors, from numbers, from morality, from religious experiences, from widespread religiosity, from propositions, from Mozart, and so on. As one might expect, there are many for atheism and agnosticism as well. Our problem is one of selection. We will not be looking at all or most of these arguments for theism but we will look at a few in some small detail. I do not plan to satisfactorily defend these arguments against all objections, many of which are very impressive. I do want to say enough to show that believing in God's existence can be a rational option for someone. We will look at arguments from the nature and order of things in this chapter and the nature and character of humanity in our next chapter.[63]

II. THE WAY THINGS MIGHT BE

---

[63] Peter Kreeft & Ronald K. Tacelli, *Handbook of Christian Apologetics*, IVP Academic; 1st Edition, 1994.

According to the great modern philosopher Sarah McLaughlin, "It's a strange world". Many thinking people cannot help but be puzzled by the very existence of the world. Even atheists sometime report that the question "Why is there something rather than nothing?" has a distinct grip on them. However, many also think that to ask such a question is illegitimate. To ask why everything exists is to ask what further thing could cause everything to exist. But if we are enquiring about a further thing we could not be inquiring about everything after all, so the question is an illegitimate totality question. However, this way of understanding the "Why" question is uncharitable. Most people seem to be aware that there are a lot of things but they appear to be diversely catagorizable. These differences may make sense of the existence of things.

It appears that the universe is a hierarchy of dynamically and systematically interacting elements, where such interactions take place between various scopes (fundamental forces, geology, astronomy), various levels (particle physics, chemistry), synchronically and diachronically (physical system formation, emergent life, reproduction, mutation and natural selection), with finely tuned constants and natural regularities that make such developments possible, a system that exists in space and time and which might not have existed. Every element in the universe can be paired with every other element and be said to exert some influence on the other while in turn being influenced by it through the media of interacting elements or directly. There is a sense in which I exert an influence on the orbit of Saturn while Saturn's mass has an influence on my motion, however slight. So the universe can be said to be the set of dyadic interactions between each pair of its elements. This may include quantum phenomena for all we know. It also includes the interaction of organisms with each other and with their environment, even where the organism is not able to sense these interactions.[64]

That the universe is a dynamic system of material elements is taken for granted by science. If science is at least an approximately reliable process of forming true judgments about things, the things it discovers confirm that the universe might be a dynamic system. If that is what the universe is, then no part of it is sufficiently self explanatory apart from the rest of the system. Of such an orderly and contingent system it clearly is legitimate to ask why it exists rather than otherwise. But what if the universe after all is not actually a dynamic system? Then the question arises, where did I get my idea of a dynamic system from? The story of how I got my idea may be complicated with a lot of intermediate steps. But whatever the ultimate source of the idea would be, it would have to be as rich and complex as my idea is to account for it adequately. So if the universe itself is not dynamic system, then something else is. Maybe it is my brain, if it is possible for me to think of a dynamic system as described above at all. So either way, I conclude that a dynamic system exists.

There are two points we will accept as rational to hold true as being among the things that we cannot not know. One is

---

[64] Walker Percy, *Lost in the Cosmos: The Last Self-Help Book*, Picador; Soft Cover edition, 2000.

that *something cannot come from nothing at all*. The other is that *whatever exists that could have otherwise not existed may have an explanation for why it is and not otherwise*. Against the first, some have said that just as zero equals +1 plus -1, nothing can yield positive matter and anti-matter. But matter plus anti-matter does not give you 'nothing'. They give you matter with zero polarity, the influence of the features of both kinds of matter cancel each other out. Against the second, as modest a claim as it is, some, like David Hume, say that things can conceivably happen with no explanation at all so the second is not intuitively a necessary truth. It is possible to imagine that you are sitting in front of an empty desk and suddenly a cat appears. According to the objection, this is just to imagine that a cat appeared without a cause. So it is conceivable that things happen without a cause and the principle is false.

But imagine you are sitting at the same desk and overhead in space the Federation Starship Enterprise teleports a cat down to the top of the desk. How is your imagination different from the previous case? So imagining a cat appearing or anything like it fails to show that it is conceivable that things happen without a cause, since there is nothing in such an imagining that necessarily indicates that it is causeless. Further, Hume's attack only has ostensive merit against the principle that whatever exists must have an explanation, but we have only insisted that it may have an explanation.[65]

---

[65] Edward Feser, *The Last Superstition: A Refutation of the New Atheism*, St. Augustine's Press; 1st edition, 2008.

III. THE CAUSE OF THE UNIVERSE

Granting that a dynamic universe exists, did it always exist? A universe that existed already from the infinite past is not possible. To make sense of why, we need to distinguish between two senses of infinity. Suppose you have a pile of beans. You could add another bean to the pile, then another, then another. It is always possible to add another bean. But this does not mean you actually at any time have an infinite number of beans no matter how many. The number of beans is always potentially infinite but not actually infinite.

But what if you actually had an infinite supply of succotash with a lima bean for each kernel of corn? If you picked out all the beans, you would have the same number of beans as the number of beans and corn you had before you picked out the beans because you could uniquely match each bean and kernel in the original pile with each bean in the new pile. But what is there that you can take half away from it and still have the same amount left? It seems that an actual infinite is impossible to realize. While there is a coherent higher mathematics of infinity, it seems to be an example of a mathematical conceptual scheme with no possible exemplification in the actual world. While a potential infinite is possible in nature, an actual infinite is not.

Suppose then that the universe then existed already for an actual infinite time. Then it would be possible that someone could have existed an actually infinite time ago. Suppose that the person is immortal and never died but kept living another day. Even so, he would never live to see the world now because his life is always a finite length long. His immortality is only a potential infinite. If that was true of the universe as a whole, it would also mean that the universe would not have made it to now. All this indicates that an actual infinite of time cannot be transversed. So the universe could not have existed for an actually infinite amount of time.

So the universe must have existed for a finite time. It must have had a beginning. But if so, it also could have had a cause (from our second principle above; if something exists, then it may have an explanation). However, the cause cannot be part of the universe because it does not exist yet before it is caused. This means that the cause is not in time also. If there is a cause, it may also have a cause other than itself. But to suppose a series of causes each explained by another cause is not a possible explanation of the cause of the universe.

Here is why. Suppose you see a caboose moving down the track and ask me how it is moving. I say that the boxcar in front of it is pulling it. But then you want to know what is pulling the boxcar. So I say that it is another boxcar. However, whether it is one or five or 5000 boxcars, it still would not explain why the caboose is moving. Similarly, a chain of causes where each cause only causes when it is being caused by another and which ends at this universe as an effect does not make a possible explanation since it would not be adequate to explain the beginning of the universe. This gives us another reason why the universe had a beginning, namely the inadequacy of positing an infinite chain of caused causes to explain any effect. So if a cause for the universe is possible, there has to be a cause that is not caused by another;

an Uncaused Cause. If there is no Uncaused Cause, then no cause of the beginning of the universe is possible. But it is possible for the beginning of the universe to have a cause; therefore that an Uncaused Cause exists that transcends the universe is possible.

Some will object that my argument is like arguing that if all the pieces of a mosaic are square, then the whole mosaic must be square, which is obviously false. They say that since I argue that if all the causes in a chain are causes that are caused by another, the chain as a whole is a cause that is caused by another. And that is to argue that the whole must have a property that all its parts have, a fallacy of composition. But such inferences are not always invalid. If someone argues that since each part of a mosaic is made of wood, then the whole mosaic is made of wood: that would be a legitimate inference. I take it that caused causes are accumulative while conserving their nature as dependent causes and so the inference is like the wood mosaic inference example. (But if a critic wanted to say that there is something that supervenes on the series of causes that is essentially different from each of the causes, something that exists as a cause of the universe which was not caused by another, that would just be to grant my conclusion anyway.)

But further, this Uncaused Cause could not itself be a random cause because such a random cause would need to be further explained and so not be an uncaused cause. Also, it could not be simple a material effect since when the conditions are right, material effects occur necessarily and efficiently. But the universe might not have existed. If the beginning of the universe was caused it was caused by something like a free choice. So we conclude that there must be an Uncaused Personal Cause for there to be an explanation for this kind of universe.[66]

IV. ETERNAL BEING

What we have just said about a series of causes apart from the universe also applies to series of changes within the universe where each change only occurs insofar as something else is causing the change (such as orbiting moons, respiration, digestion, climate change, the exploding matter of the Big Bang, and so on). In order for those changes to have a possible explanation, there must be an Unchanged Changer by the same reasoning as in the case of causes.

Similarly, if the universe exists, something must have existed for eternity. Why is that? If at any time in the past nothing had existed, then nothing would exist now since something cannot come from nothing. So if nothing existed no explanation of the universe would be possible. But the universe contains features that come into being and become degenerate, which is to say they are contingent with respect to time. For contingent things, there is always a time when they do not exist. But if everything in the universe were contingent, then it is physically possible that there was a time when nothing existed.

Notice that *I did not say* that since for everything that existed there is a time that it did not exist, then there *must be* time

---

[66] William Lane Craig, *Reasonable Faith: Christian Truth and Apologetics*, Crossway; 3rd edition, 2008 (See also Moreland, *Scaling the Secular City*).

when everything did not exist. That everyone has a mother does not imply there is a mother who is mother to everyone. But it is clearly possible though not necessary that if everything does not exist at a time, a time *may be* where nothing exists. However, since universe exists, then there must not have been a time when nothing existed. That there was never a time that nothing existed may have an explanation by our second principle. But the only thing that could possibly explain why there never was a time when nothing existed is if not everything in history was a contingent thing which had a time that it did not exist. So if the existence of the universe has an adequate explanation, it must be that there exists something such that there is no time that it does not exist, a Thing which exists at all times, an Eternal Thing. So if contingent things exist, than an Eternal thing is possible.[67]

If then there is something that exists at all times, what could explain it? It's possible that it depends on something else for its existence, which in turn depends on something further for its existence. But again it would not be enough that there is an infinite chain of eternal things that depend on other eternal things to explain the existence of the original eternal thing, just like there couldn't be such a chain of caused causes to explain changes in the beginning of the universe. So if an eternal thing is possible there must be an eternal thing that does not need to be explained by another to possibly explain it.

---

[67] Samuel Clarke, *Discourse on the Being and Attributes of God*, R. Griffin and Company, 1823.

So it is possible that there is something that does not begin or cease to exist and that does not depend on anything else for its existence, an Independent Eternal Being.

V. THE END OF THE UNIVERSE

Suppose you were coming into Syracuse, New York by car and you saw a bunch of rocks on a hillside that spelled "The Ancient Order of the Hibernians Welcomes You to the Emerald City!" you might conclude that some folks are giving you a greeting. But if you thought that the rocks actually fell down from the sky at random during a meteor shower, then you would not think there was any message at all. Even though it looks like a message, it would just be one of the possible ways rocks could fall at random. One cannot think both that it was merely a random distribution and there was a message from someone. A merely random explanation is not a possible explanation for a message.[68]

Furthermore, if you are playing Bridge and it turns out that everyone had a perfect bridge hand - all thirteen cards in the same suit - you are likely going to say that the dealer cheated. Though you know it is possible on a random deal, you would say that if everyone got a perfect hand, then the dealer most likely cheated, even before the cars are dealt. And though the dealer does not deal any cards from the bottom of the deck, you would still say that he might have stacked the deck before dealing. He

---

[68] Richard Taylor, *Metaphysics*, Prentice Hall; 4th edition, 1991.

did not need to alter the mechanics of the dealing to target the desired result. This illustrates that direct manipulation into the mechanics of a process is not necessary for design to be involved or detected.

Suppose for the sake of argument that the universe developed through time using natural mechanisms including mutation and natural selection in a dynamic system. Such a system would also be symbiotic since organisms interacting with their environment are part of the system, so that the system includes both extrinsic and mechanical, and intrinsic and vital interactions. This would not be possible if this happened merely at random. Why not? In such a system, each thing is dependent on each other thing directly or remotely. No part sufficiently explains itself. It must be understood in terms of the system and its role in it. As a system, the elements function as parts in a whole that is greater than the individual elements themselves. If there is an explanation for all this, it cannot be found in any of the components individually or aggregately. It must be prior to the whole. But that can only be if the cause transcends the whole system as the unifying efficiency.

Further, the explanation must have the whole system already existing as a guide to the creation of the system. This is possible if the Cause is an intelligent Being which is able to entertain the scheme of the universe as an already complete idea, like a designer. If we thought that the universe was the result of a blind process, we could not think of it as a genuinely dynamic system, just as we could not think random rocks had a message for us. However, the systematic character of the universe is the presupposed object of scientific inquiry. Without it, there is nothing that science would seek. So if the universe exists as a system, then a transcendent intelligent cause is possible.[69]

Besides these attempts at demonstrating the possibility of God's existence, there are inductive arguments from various notions of design; order, purpose (either beneficent or non-beneficent), emerging value, emerging complexity, emerging life and reproduction, emerging "information", fine-tuning, beauty etc. These can all be cast as arguments in the form of inference to the best explanation. Here's an example of how inference to the best explanation works. Species perpetuate through reproduction, either by osmosis or sexual reproduction, which is a process in which everything has to be fitted just right to work, such as the woman's placenta which allows nutrients from the mother's bloodstream to pass into the baby's blood stream and allows waste from the baby's blood stream into the mother's without mingling the blood of the two. The system is necessary because the baby could have a different blood type than the mother and their blood mixing could be fatal. A Designer who is involved in the world as an ultimate cause would explain how such a process could happen in just the right way to assure survival of the species and it is a better explanation than its known rivals. So it is reasonable to think such a Designer exists. Notice that this argument has the form or schema:

---

[69] W. Norris Clarke, SJ, *The Creative Retrieval of Thomas Aquinas: Essays in Thomistic Philsophy, New and Old*, Fordham University Press; 3rd edition, 2009.

(1) E.

(2) H explains E.

(3) H is the best explanation for E.

(4) Thus, it is likely to be true that H.

"E" is some event or evidence to be explained and "H" is some proposed hypothesis that explains E. Conditions (1) – (3) have to be satisfied to justify (4). The argument does not demonstrate its conclusion but only gives reasons to accept it as true rather than not. The argument can still provide a basis for moral certainty even if the conclusion is not absolutely secure, if the support for the conditions is significantly high.

The schema helps us sort out possible attacks on the argument. Let E represent the event of reproduction and H represent the Designer Hypothesis. One could object to (1) by saying there really is no special process called reproduction since after all like everything else it's just matter rearranging particles in the flux of time and thus there are no "kinds" of processes such as "reproduction". This is an extremely counter intuitive view and forces one to think that biology is like interpreting an ink blot with our own projected impressions.

Another objection would be against (2). The designer hypothesis fails to explain sufficiently because we have never seen anyone design a reproductive system in the way we have seen people design watches or cars. Also, the emergence of reproduction in the universe is unique so we have nothing to compare to it to base an analogy to anything for purposes of explanation. In response, neither of these conditions is necessary for an adequate explanation since we see science postulate unseen entities (such as quarks) and hypotheses for unique situations (such as the Big Bang) all the time.

An objection to (3) is that it commits the "God of the Gaps fallacy"; it infers a spooky cause which we could not verify or falsify only because we don't know how something could happen otherwise. However, the Design Hypothesis at its best construal is based on what we do know, not what we do not know. According to our concept of what material objects are, there is no reasonable expectation that such a system as reproduction is likely to emerge at random. Even assuming a series of different paths of accumulating gradual changes in non-reproductive forms converged in just the right way to form a working placenta, it would be as adequate an explanation as if a bomb went off in a junkyard and the explosion produced a Trans Am. Just like the case of the perfect bridge hand, it is possible but not reasonable to expect such a hand assuming the dealer did not cheat. It is more likely to expect one assuming the dealer did.

Another objection to (3) would be that naturalistic evolution is a better explanation than a Designer. However, species evolution presupposes the transmission of naturally selected genes and genetic information from one generation to its successor generation. So reproduction is required to make species evolution possible, and thus evolution cannot explain reproduction. The evolution defender could reply that it is not necessary that reproduction appear all at once for evolution to occur. The evolution of reproduction could have taken several steps where at each step only a partial reproductive process occurred, enough to carry forward some information into the next stage of development. This "proto-reproductive processes" bootstrap to evolution seems to be guilty of equivocating between being "reproductive of a little" with being "a little reproductive". The appearance of reproduction may have taken various forms over natural history but remains just as complex in each case.[70]

Using the schema of inference to the best explanation, one can develop several arguments from various concepts of design like the ones mentioned and anticipate criticisms in order to answer them. Not all will be equally compelling but several will hold up very well.[71]

VI.   ABSOLUTE BEING

To summarize, science presupposes and seems to confirm that the universe we have discovered is a dynamic system as well as a contingent system that began to exist. Since that is true, a universe that is a contingent dynamic system of material elements has a possible explanation, then there is a possible explanation, according to our principle that an adequate explanation for whatever exists is possible. But there could not be an adequate explanation for such a universe, unless an uncaused cause, an independent eternal being, and a transcendent creative intellect exist and that would be adequately explained if there existed One

---

[70] Smart and Haldane, *Great Debates in Philosophy*.
[71] William A. Dembski, *The Design Inference: Eliminating Chance through Small Probabilities* (Cambridge Studies in Probability, Induction, and Decision Theory), Cambridge University Press, 1998.

Being that was all of these things. Therefore, it is possible that there is one being independently existing that is the ultimate cause and the intelligent designer of the dynamic and contingent universe.

However, how could such a being be possible? If a being is an independent being, it does not depend on anything else for existence. If such a being did not exist, nothing could bring it into existence, and therefore its existence would be impossible. Since we have just argued that an independent being is possible, it must be the case that it exists. So therefore, an independent being exists that is the first cause and intelligent designer of the universe. Since an independent being that fulfils the roles of cause and designer exists, what could make such an independent existence possible, unless it is a being that is absolutely self-explanatory. Thus, a self-explanatory being is possible, but again that could only be because there is a self-explanatory being, since no other source of explanation could be a condition of its existence.

It is possible that these are one and the same being. Also, it is possible that this being is an absolute being. An absolute being is a being that none greater can be conceived. Whatever makes something good, the absolute being has it perfectly by definition. Thus it is unlimited, one, perfect, omnipotent, eternal, and prior in reality to all other beings. Such a being would be absolutely autonomous in its existence such that its existence is possibly explained by itself. Thus I cannot think of the absolutely perfect being without thinking of it as possibly self-explanatory.

Therefore, an Absolute Being that is self-explanatory (or metaphysically necessary) exists that is the principal intelligent cause of our universe. Here we can simply add that this being is what we call God. We may further infer some of the attributes of God. He is the ultimate source of all change in the universe but also the source of His own being and thus all powerful. Since he is ultimately self-explanatory, he is eternal. Since He is the principal source of explanation for the system of the universe He is intelligent. But since the universe might not have existed, bringing it into existence was something neither determined by a blind necessity (since it might not have existed) nor did it come about by mere chance (since the universe has an explanation). This argues that the universe came into being by something like arbitrated choice. This suggests that the principal source of the universe, being both intelligent and arbitrary, is a Personal Agent. An Absolute and Personal God exists.

VII. CONCLUSION: THE GOD OF THE PHILOSOPHERS

The Absolute/Personal Being exists and this is what we all mean by "God". These arguments do not tell us much about the Being that exists, only that (and here I drop the conventions) He is and that he caused the world and its design and that He transcends the world He caused. Even our concept of an absolute and personal being cannot give us a complete and comprehensive concept of God. The being remains incomprehensible but apprehensible, like the notion of infinity itself. It must be recalled that many of our biblically based concepts of God (Creator, Redeemer, Savior, and Father) also do not say more than that there is something that created us, something that redeemed us, something that saved us and something that is like a Father to us. This is not to say what it is that has these relations to us. The Mystery of God's being remains in both natural and special revelation.

This is the "God of the philosophers". If we recall what we said earlier about the distinction between knowing and showing, this account may not even succeed in telling us everything creation tells about God, much less all that God reveals about Himself in Scripture. But it does show enough to establish conditions that make the prior probability of Christian Theology more plausible. It establishes that there is indeed an object for study for the science of theology.

12. Homo Pietas

To quote another philosopher, Jim Morrison, "People are strange". Besides the wonderful features of the universe that suggest a Personal Intelligent and Absolute First Cause, there are also features about ourselves, immediately apparent to ourselves that suggest a personal, morally perfect Cause as well. As Paul says, all have the Law of God written on their hearts. We want to focus on the uniqueness of humans as a ground for belief in God.

I. TWO WORLDVIEWS AND A QUESTION

When I was in an assistant in graduate school, I helped a professor teach a standard introduction course in philosophy, using mostly contemporary texts to discuss the big questions such as whether knowledge, God, the soul, free will, or the meaning of life existed. At the end of the course, he summarized the various answers we discussed in two columns, indicating that they could be understood as two coherent total philosophies. His list looked something like this (see Figure):

Worldview Question	Naturalist's Answers	Theist'sAnswers
Ultimate Reality	Physical Facts	God
Knowledge	Sciences Only	Universals Also
Human Nature	Matter Only	Soul and Body
Free Will	Physically Determined	Person Determined
Meaning of Life	Subjectively Created	Objective Purpose

Call the collection of views in the middle column the Naturalistic Worldview and the last column the Theistic Worldview. Also, each of the views on the Naturalism side are "nothing but" views, just as Naturalism as a worldview is a "nothing but" view. That means that in each case, the answer is always that there is nothing else but what the view says is available. For example, Materialism says that the mind is either nothing but matter or non-existent, and subjectivism says that meaning is nothing but a subjectively created value or there is no meaning. The alternative views on the Theistic side, deny the "nothing but" claims. For example, Dualism affirms the material brain but denies that the mind is nothing but the brain. Also, Theism accepts that meaning is subjective in the sense that it must be realized in the life of a person but not that it is nothing but subjective – it exists as an objectively discovered purpose. One must evaluate their subjective grasp on meaning by an objective standard for the sake of meaning itself.

This is related to the type of arguments given for the various positions on both sides. In each case, the basic strategy for the Naturalist is to show that nothing more than the physical and the material is necessary to adequately explain the phenomena the question tries to understand. For example, the physical determinist may argue that we can explain our experience of deliberative choice as nothing but our organism slewing to a stable equilibrium between competing desires. The Theistic alternative argues that there are features of deliberation that the "nothing but" explanation fails to explain. For example, personal determinists argue that free actions of the will differ absolutely from other events because other events just happen while actions always are done for a purpose or aim. But since an equilibrium state of an organism is just an event that happens, it cannot be identical to an action. Events are not essentially and intrinsically directed to an end but actions are. This gives you a sense of how these debates tend to go. We however are not going into such debates but instead stake everything on the big picture.

It seems my professor was warranted in thinking that such views do tend to stand or fall together. Try to imagine embracing all but one issue on either list. The other views undermine the prior likelihood of the exception. Trying to embrace only half of one worldview is an unstable position, just as we saw in the case of different views of the meaning of life in Chapter 6. So with this, we will treat the stable versions as potentially viable views.

II. CHOOSING MY OWN WORLDVIEW

Coming back to my professor's summary, he then asked the class how they would compare the two. One student said that the naturalistic view was based on reason while the theistic view was based on faith. She was satisfied that the theistic view in the course had failed to pass the bar as a credible view. This seemed too uncharitable to another student who offered that both views had evidence to support them but that naturalism had more evidence. Of course, that meant one ought to hold naturalism rather than theism. So either way it was a bad day for theism.

But if we are to take seriously the question of which view to choose for ourselves, we need to ask what this means. We are being asked in a face to face situation what we ought to hold as true, a choice to be determined based on obliging principles of weighing reasons and for which we can be held responsible. In such a situation, as thinking and choosing participants in a dialogue, we cannot but take the situation seriously, but doing so is quite natural for us and not onerous.

Such a state of affairs presupposes several conditions being the case of which we can only survey a few. (1) It supposes that we have personal access to reasons and evidence which are able to move us intrinsically according to their content. (2) It assumes that our thoughts and choices have objects that they are about, even about worldviews. (3) It assumes that we are the same persons throughout the course of deliberation, that we have not been substituted with someone else so that the person who knows the answer is not a different person from the person who began to weigh the evidence. (4) It assumes that we are really obliged in the choice that we make and that we can be held responsible for doing otherwise. Finally, (5) it assumes that the basis of making the choice has to do with one or the other being more true, which implies that there must be some correspondence possible between what we think is the case and what is the case.

III. THEISM AND RATIONAL CHOICE

Given that personal worldview choice has these assumed commitments, is the theistic worldview a possible option? Suppose theism is true. Then the cause of the universe and the cause of the human knower is the same intelligent cause as we saw in

Chapter 10. As we saw in chapters 2 and 3, such a cause would make the universe to exist with a nature designed to serve some specific ends which would be an intelligible nature. He could also create finite knowers that are not merely passive experiencers of the world but have minds whose nature is made to discern and perceive the order of things. Just as a computer designer pre-formats the computer and printer so that they can communicate with each other, so God could "pre-format" the human mind to recognize the intelligible structure of the world. This makes an identity between thought and world possible; our concepts are the same form as the natures of things. This is an extension of the design inference we made in the last chapter. As we said, if I see rocks on the hillside that seem to say "Welcome to Syracuse" but think that they just happened to be there by chance, I could not construe it as someone having a message for me. It turns out this applies to the whole body of knowledge we think we derive about the world. If I thought my thoughts about the world were actually just brute stimuli in the brain, I could not see them as making sense or referring to anything in reality.

Further, if God exists, then it is not necessarily true that everything is material, including ourselves. If materialism is true, then it is hard to account for identity over time. We see ourselves as enduring units. Imagine an old wooden clipper ship. At first, it is brand new. But as each board is damaged it gets replaced by a new board. At some point, all the boards have been replaced. Is it the same ship? What if we saved all the old boards that we replaced and rebuilt the ship? Would that be the same ship as the original one? When speaking of strictly material parts there seems to be no fact of the matter about the identity of the ship. But we replace nearly all of our cells and tissues several times during an average life. To be the same person as before, we need to be more than just cells and tissues.

This is possible if God exists, since that means that other immaterial substances may also exist that are true units and not mere aggregates of physical components. Such an immaterial soul may be subject to being influenced by content of reasons and evidence over time, rather than being redistributed by mechanical interaction, such as when we say we were compelled by the evidence. Being rationally persuaded also includes being guided by norms and objective aims such as sufficient evidence, logical validity, and truth. These exert a peculiar kind of normative force on the mind and also the conscience. Seeing to it that we are following a norm of thinking requires a kind of foresight that we do not attribute to blind interacting parts. Finally, such a trans-physical intelligent substance could be an agent moved by reason rather than having behavior that is determined by the natural laws and causes from outside the person's own reason and will. It could be the source of original choices of its own. And as the cause of those choices, it can meaningfully be held responsible for them.[72]

So if Theism is true, rational choice from between worldviews can be real and meaningful. It makes sense to ask a

---

[72] Gary Habermas and J. P. Moreland, *Beyond Death: Exploring the Evidence for Immortality*, Wipf & Stock Publishers, 2004.

person to make a rational choice between worldviews in a theistic world.

IV. NATURALISM AND RATIONAL CHOICE

On the other hand, if naturalism is true then thought is a behavior of the body or brain. Even if that behavior can be characterized as following a sophisticated pattern that coordinates certain inputs from the environment to certain outputs either into the environment or into the brain itself, it remains true that such behavior is the result of the regular operation of natural laws on the physical organism. It is the mechanism of the brain necessarily, efficiently, and physically causing the subsequent states of the brain and the behavior of the organism. Even where it is granted that the organism may have felt experiences, these are just spooky aggregated by-products. They do not in turn have any real effect on the organism or its environment, nor do they endure through time or constitute a true unity.

If this is so, all of my beliefs are also products of the physical process. My beliefs are understood to be beliefs about the world and what is in it. But it is difficult to imagine how this could be true of material states. One way to capture this idea is to contrast beliefs with organic states in their relations with other natural objects. We observed last time that the world was a dynamic system that could be explained as interactions between any two of the objects in it, like the gravitational influence between Saturn and me. This is true of all the physical objects in the universe.

But thoughts and language are different from this. These are not understood as a response to a stimulus, which would be an interaction between two objects. Rather they are understood to represent something to the thinker, speaker, and listener. There is always something we are thinking about or talking about. The relationship of representation is not a dyadic interaction but rather an irreducibly "triadic" relation (A represents B to C). The three point connection between thought, thinker, and object is intrinsic, that is, the relations between the points could not exist in the absence of any one of them. Thus, representation cannot be explained by the interactions between the organism, its brain state, and the physical object, since these can be analyzed into the extrinsic interaction between each of them, as well as between them and all other physical objects, which would go on even if any one of them were absent from the others.

Some will say that by studying the brain and its environment when we use representations, we will know what really is happening when we say that we are having a thought or using language, and then see that the representation "just is' the physical interactions going on at that time. While it is certainly expected that some such physical interaction is happening while I have a thought, the correlation of my thought to my brain's behavior is not necessarily because they are identical. Further, since the brain is interacting with the environment when I am not thinking (such as in sleep) and since the description of such behavior is essentially the same in character as when I am thinking, there is no criterion for picking out which interactions count as my thoughts and which do not. It is not clear how representation could have arisen out of a purely physical system. But in order to speak meaningfully about rational worldview choice we must be able to think about the world.[73]

Some object and say that it is possible to make sense of representation physically because that is that we do when we say that the rings of a tree trunk represent the age of the tree. But the ring formation process is a completely physical process. Also, when we go to the store and pick up a can of peas, when the cashier slides the wand tip across the bar code, the machine displays the figure "CAN OF PEAS .... $.69". It is clear that it is representing the truth that the can of peas is for sale at sixty-nine cents, yet the process by which it operates is completely dyadic and mechanical. However, neither case is a case of original representation. For example, if I say to you "Polly wants a cracker", I am saying that Polly the parrot wants a cracker. But if Polly the parrot says "Polly wants a cracker", she is not saying that Polly wants a cracker, in fact she's not saying that anything is the case at all. She is simply responding with an audio signal cultivated by us to sound like an intelligible sentence but which to her is simply a conditioned reflex to give when she is hungry.

Similarly, the machine is not saying that a can of peas is sixty-nine cents nor is the tree trunk saying that it is X years old by the formation of X rings over the years. Both are cases of the use made of machines by people who are capable of forming representations by using physical objects and processes as symbols for themselves. In the case of the cash machine, the machine

---

[73] Walker Percy, *Message in a Bottle*.

is designed to transmit signals in the form of a preselected set of pixels on a screen which are arranged to look like symbols about the groceries to symbol users, the cashier and shopper. In the case of the tree trunk, a pre-existing process has been designated to serve as a representation by people because of the utility of the phenomena to serve as symbol for data about the tree. The meaningfulness of the rings and the pixels on the register is derived from the human capacity to form beliefs and representations about things and is not original to the physical attributes of either. The representations we find in trees, machines, computers, and books are all derived from original symbol users and if these symbol users ceased to exist, these would become meaningless. But if materialism is true, everything is a machine from top to bottom and there could not have been any original symbol users. Nothing would mean anything. There must be original irreducible representation somewhere for there to be any derived representation anywhere. If naturalism is true, there is neither.

Also, as we saw in the previous chapter, if I were to believe anything, including the belief that I believed something based on compelling evidence, that belief must be explained as an effect of the physical processes occurring within the organism. Suppose I'm an overzealous evangelist who is also a super duper brain scientist. I develop a pill such that if anyone takes it, they form the belief that the existence and structure of the cosmos convinces them to believe in a divine creator, that historical evidences compel them to think that Christianity is true. This pill dissolves in liquid and has no taste. All I do as an evangelist is go to bars and drop these pills into the customers' drinks. Then they suddenly become Christians and I have a great contract with Zondervan Christian Books and Pfizer Pharmaceutical. But we would say that, after all, the victims of my pill are not justified in believing that Christianity was proven true in these conditions, because the cause of their belief was a result only of physical forces acting within the brain and not based on the intrinsic force of the evidence.

But if naturalism is true, then this would be the case with all of everyone's beliefs, including the naturalist's belief in naturalism. So if naturalism is true, the naturalist's belief in naturalism is not justified nor could he really rationally persuade someone else to be a naturalist. In this sense naturalism is self-stultifying and unlivable. Suppose it could be that the naturalist can give an argument with premises and naturalistic conclusion that is valid and based on facts that support the premises. According to the naturalist view, this would be like a computer with an artificial intelligence program. But the validity and evidential relations would still be otiose in the story of how this came about in the mind of the naturalist if naturalism is true. The machine does not see that the facts validly support the conclusion. In spite of appearances, it would not make sense to say that the naturalist was persuaded by the specific features of the reasoning or evidence that intrinsically support the conclusion. So if naturalism is true, it would not be rational to be a naturalist.[74]

---

[74] Edward Feser, *Philosophy of Mind (A Beginner's Guide)*, Oneworld; Revised edition, 2007.

This also applies to the choice to believe in naturalism by the naturalist. The naturalist might say that believing in naturalism counts as his free choice because it was something he wanted to do and nothing kept him from doing it. When you look around that is all anyone really means when they say they acted freely. But again, think about the salvation pill. Let us add that besides making you think there's a proof for Christianity it also makes you want to be a Christian. Would we say that when the barfly became a Christian, since he or she did what he or she wanted to do without hindrance that he or she acted freely? It seems not. But if naturalism is true, forces in nature beyond our control determined all our wants and so none of our decisions can be said to be free. And if not free, then we cannot be said to be responsible for making them since our own persons were not the original source of our choice.

Also, we could not be obliged because we could not make sense of moral judgments. If naturalism is true then all facts are physical facts. Thus if there are moral facts they are just among the physical facts. Maybe they are facts about the behavioral states of human organisms. Maybe they are physical states of affairs such as where most creatures experience the least pain or where creatures are most successful in adapting to their environment.

However, it is not clear how any set of physical descriptions can be construed as an "ought". If I recommend this possible state of physical facts to any other possible state of physical facts, it is hard to see that as anything more than expressing my tastes. Questions like "Why should I seek to bring about the greatest good for the greatest number?" or "Why shouldn't I win a person's trust to get them in a vulnerable spot, then kill them and take their stuff?" do not seem to have a possible answer if the only kind of fact I can appeal to is another physical fact. Nor is there an answer to: "Which worldview ought I to hold based on reasons and evidence?" But if God exists and the universe was a result of His creative work, we can ask questions about the good purpose nature was designed for, because we may see that nature really would be for something, including human nature. These considerations also apply to other normative judgments, such as the norms I use when deciding between worldviews.

V. COGITO ERGO DUES EST

Coming back to my professor, I conclude that the only two choices to the question "Which view, naturalism or theism, is the most rational to hold", I answer that the only possible answer is theism. Only theism makes a rational worldview choice possible, while naturalism cannot consistently be chosen. If I am to take the question seriously and not see it as a kind of facon de parler, then theism is the only available answer. When I think about the question – which is just to be thinking – I cannot not take it seriously. Therefore God exists.

One obvious objection is that none of this shows that naturalism is false. It could be that the drama of asking questions is just a useful fiction for orienting the mind to its environment as a natural object and not to be taken literally. Just because a naturalist cannot be taken seriously when he tries to justify naturalism,

naturalism could still be true. But part of the answer to that is, if the question is not to taken seriously, then we are free to believe whatever we want if we can, true or not. We are not obliged to give a justification for our belief that theism is true and naturalism false. If the naturalist thinks that is irresponsible then he's taking the question seriously again. The naturalist cannot have it both ways. Since whatever I believe is the result of natural laws and physical events, I cannot be obliged to do otherwise, since I could not have done otherwise. All education becomes indoctrination and conditioning. All politics becomes therapy.[75]

Another objection the naturalist might raise is that Theism is too queer. It postulates a transcendent God, an immaterial soul that is an agent that rises above the causal order of the physical laws, nonnatural properties like substantial units, intrinsic ends, intentions, and moral facts, and other kinds of causes besides mechanical ones, like rational causation and volitional causation. All of this metaphysical litter is weird and spooky. Furthermore, why should it be that in the vast cosmos we should only find these strange features – man being the strangest – only on this planet? This looks like a case of cosmic special pleading.

However, this really does not amount to an argument against theism. It amounts rather to saying that the trouble with nonnatural properties is that they are nonnatural, and does nothing more than express distaste for them, rather than a reason for them not to exist. As to cosmic special pleading, the plausibility for

---

[75] Francis A. Schaeffer, *Back to Freedom and Dignity*, Hodder & Stoughton Ltd, 1973.

this arises because of distaste for the metaphysical perspective. Psalm 8 illustrates this. The psalmist is meditating on the cosmos and asks "what is man that Thou art mindful of him?" which expresses man's smallness against the vastness of the universe. But then he shifts perspective and says "You have made him a little lower than the angels". The psalmist can see man's place in the hierarchy of being. In terms of the space and location that man takes up, it appears insignificant. But man also has a position somewhere along a metaphysical continuum from particles, elements, plants, animals on one side and angels and archangels and God on the other. From that point of view, man's place is not odd. As Pascal expressed it, man is a reed that is easily crushed by the universe. But that which is crushed is still greater than that which crushes it because man is a thinking reed.

In his great essay "Meditation in a Tool Shed", C.S. Lewis describes being inside a shed where a beam of light comes in through a hole in the roof. One can look at the light and see an indistinctly white beam in a dark tool shed. But if one stands with one's eye in the light and looks along the beam, one can see the blue sky, clouds, and the leaves of the trees nearby. One can look at the beam and look along the beam but not both at the same time. Each is a comprehensive perspective but each only tells part of the whole story so that we need to both look at and look along.[76]

---

[76] From C. S. Lewis, *God in the Dock: Essays in Theology and Ethics*, Wm. B. Eerdmans Publishing Co., 1972.

The same may be said of man and the cosmos. We may take the perspective of the spectator and look at the cosmos and man and describe the visible goings on in a perspective neutral way as we do in science. Science provides a comprehensive picture of the visible physical universe. But we can also look along man and see the cosmos from the perspective of a participant who thinks and chooses. Naturalism shows an exclusive preference for the spectator perspective. But man the spectator is the same as man the participant. Furthermore, it is only through persons as participants that the natural world receives the language used to describe it and becomes an object of science, so that the ability of having a robust scientific perspective depends essentially on the participant perspective.

Naturalism turns out to be a skeptical hypothesis like the hypothesis that we are living in the Matrix or being deceived by an evil demon. According to the naturalist, the participant perspective, with the way it tracks intentions, purposes, universals, and other queer would-be features is at best a heuristic that points to the things that science needs to explain or explain away. But then why stop there? Why is it not the case that natural science with its descriptions of natural laws and physical interactions is just a heuristic for the sequencing and spatial distribution of free standing patches of sensation with no causal connection between them a la Hume and Kant? On such an approach, which would be a kind of scientific nonrealism, there is not even a real mechanical explanation for the world and no deeper point in doing science than to provide a phenomenal description of the appearance of the "as-if" universe. If the naturalist replies that the value of science makes it worth the gamble of rejecting this for scientific realism, the reply is that by parity of reasoning the proposed benefits of accepting the participant perspective make it much more worth the gamble of rejecting the naturalistic hypothesis for the sake of the participant perspective. A realistic naturalism seems to be explanatorily unstable, tending either to an impressionistic nihilism or to theism.

Against this last claim, the naturalist objects that appeal to the participant perspective is a "science stopper". If the defender of the participant perspective agrees that science is valuable, they should reject their point of view because it would stop the search for material causes by substituting other kinds of causes (mental causes, volitional causes) and thus prevents science from growing. In reply, we would say that the appeal to non-physical causes is not motivated by ignorance of physical causes but by the knowledge of the participant perspective. Within it, we see properties that cannot be accounted for physically. Also, what the participant perspective shows us are ultimate causes and ultimate ends. Natural operational science is about the study of intermediate causes and instrumental ends. Consequently, the participant perspective does not infringe on the domain of science, but rather supplements it.

The fact that we are even discussing this at all shows we are already committed to taking rational choice seriously. Therefore, God exists. To borrow a bit from Descartes, cogito ergo Deus est. I think, therefore God exists.

VI. CONSCIENCE AND COMMON CONSENT

I want to finish with two more arguments. We have been looking at the role that God has in making the universe intelligible and making human beings such that they may study and understand it. We have also given an account about how humanity may come to know about God. We have also seen how moral responsibility plays a role in inquiry in the form of normative judgments about what is true.

But humans are more than just knowers. They are makers and doers who are involved in creative and practical concerns, which involve making judgments of the good and the right as well as of the truth. As we saw in chapter 2, one of the objections to theism is the problem of why God seems to allow so much evil without any apparent justification. But to make sense of this as an objection presupposes having some criteria for distinguishing good from evil and for distinguishing between justified and unjustified evil. This would just be to have access to an objective standard of good and evil.

Such a standard would be universal, at least in the sense that there are some basic criteria that are always true, such as that one should do good and not do evil. Even if what those criteria would require in the unique concrete situations in which moral choices must be made has to be adapted to the context of the choice, they have a comprehensive relevance to all possible situations. As we suggested, moral laws could not be physical facts. So if there are universal moral laws, they must be non-physical truths. Further they must be true concerning human beings, since they must live by them, but not be a mere product of human invention, since they are not revisable all the way down. This is best explained by a non-human personal agency as the source of law, namely a Lawgiver. And this we call God. So the problem of evil objection against God's existence needs God to exist to make sense of it.[77]

In reply to this, the critics can say that when they imply a transcendent principle of good and evil, they are only presupposing it for the sake of argument, just as they are only presupposing that God is all knowing and all good for the sake of argument. Still to do this, they must objectively know what the difference is between good and evil to refute God's existence by appealing to an actual injustice. This must not be mere presupposition. The critics may reply that they are simply projecting what an absolute good must be like from some actual preference that people happen to have. But such a procedure would then not be able to assure us that we have found a real contradiction in God's goodness because we could not be assured that what we found was really good or bad.

The critics may then reply that one can find a contradiction by appealing to God's own stated preferences or what so called followers of God say is right or wrong, and then finding something that happens that contradicts that. However, in the context of questioning God at all, rather than some person or another's take on God, the only thing that we could appeal to for God's view of right or wrong is what God does, which is just

---

[77] C.S. Lewis, *Mere Christianity*, Harper San Francisco, 2001.

what happens. Then the argument would never get off the ground. Everything would be good all the time and no problem of evil would exist.

Finally, the critic could affirm cultural relativism and just simply attack the idea of any objective moral truth by saying that no need exists to introduce it. The actual diversity of moral opinions throughout the world shows that there is no consensus about what is and is not moral. What is moral is just what is accepted as such by a community. An answer to this is that this diversity is reasonably expected by two features of objective moral truth; (1) such truth must be adapted to circumstances as we said before and the world cultures are diverse just because their local and historical circumstances are diverse, and (2) it is possible to be wrong about what the moral laws are. However, cultural relativism is inadequate just because some moral propositions, just like Augustine's truths we cannot not know, are known to be true. For example, it is wrong to torture babies for the fun of it.[78]

An important difference between moral knowledge and other kinds of inquiry is that moral reflection is not merely a detached project. We discover when we consider moral judgments of approval or disapproval, that they are attached to very strong feelings, affections, and passions. The capacity for moral judgment, which we have come to call conscience, seems to exist from the beginning of consciousness although it clearly goes through development as our capacity to think grows. We seem to

---

[78] Moreland, *Scaling the Secular City*.

be aware that we always pursue what we take to be good. But we are also aware of a strong tendency to choose the bird in the hand over the two in the bush even though we know that two is better than one. Conscience seems to be our natural equipment for compensating for that tendency by goading us to do what we would not otherwise prefer to do. Surprisingly, conscience is already with us, as if anticipating the existence of weakness of will.

When we go against our conscience, we experience strong feelings of self-disapproval that contradict what our preferences were at the time we made the choice. These experiences seem to track with moral judgments and not judgments of taste. Matters of taste do not seem to involve the strong feelings of disapproval that go with a betrayed conscience. Conscience is an interior judge. Further, because these feelings go against our preferences at the time and have a moral force, it seems to us like conscience is the voice of another in our soul. Conscience is contingent in many ways but we can speak of a healthy and proper functioning conscience as opposed to a hardened, insensitive, or missing conscience. There seems to be a fact of the matter about how the conscience is supposed to work.[79]

Thus, conscience is also a pointer to God. Unlike the other arguments that we have been looking act so far, conscience is a more immediate indicator of God to us from within. We do not simply conclude about God at the end of an argument. We are directly in His presence by means of the interior judge which

---

[79] John Henry Newman, *Grammar of Assent*, 1870.

declares the Voice of God, warning against transgressions, condemning moral failures, and requiring restitution and atonement for wrongs done as the price of the return of peace of mind. While other arguments for God's existence provide a hygienic support for the proper function of conscience and the direct awareness of God in it, conscience returns the favor by providing a direct acquaintance of the Judge of the universe for each person.

Finally, a common argument for God's existence is the argument from common consent. Belief in God in some sense or another is more than significantly present among the total population of mankind. Canaanite religion as described in the Old Testament is a fairly typical case. There one finds belief in one absolute but remote God which has nothing so much to do except create and sustain the world and many minor deities who must be manipulated to get results desired. Many cultures have at least a henotheistic system of mythology such as the ancient Koreans, the Philippine Aborigines, and Egypt under the reformer Anknaton. A most likely explanation for this is that humans have a natural tendency to form beliefs about God unless prevented by circumstances like growing up in a secular technologically developed society. Reviewing these and the arguments from Chapter 6 and Chapter 11, the connections we have drawn between man as a knower, a thinker, a speaker, a desirer, and a responsible chooser, we can understand this tendency. All this suggests that forming a belief in God is a natural end for our species. We were made for God.

VII. FROM GOD TO CHRIST

This concludes our efforts for the time being to show why it's reasonable to believe that God exists. At this point we are going to just plump it here and say that there is a Divine Creator who created the cosmos in all its complexity and created humans with reason, rational appetites, and the power to choose. God is an Absolute Personal Eternal Agent whose essence is to exist. We have argued for a beginning to the universe and for the possibility of origin science, but we have also argued enough that even if one assumes an infinitely long history of the universe and evolution, God still must exist. While each argument provides a case for theism, each of them contributes support for the prior plausibility of the others, leading to a cumulative moral certainty that includes a certainty of a direct awareness of God. We have not argued for a recent creation or any Christian doctrine of the world based on Scripture. Rather the theism we have argued for is what we think reason best judges the world to be apart from any special knowledge God may have given beyond what God shows us about Himself in nature. If anything that God may choose to make known revises the best conclusions reason can manage, that should not be surprising.

However, what we have argued for is enough to guide us in judging the prior probability of the Christian hypothesis in examining the special evidences for Christianity. God's existence determines what we take to be likely and unlikely to be the case in the world. This sets up an objectively argued plausibility structure for arguing for the historical reality of special revelation.

13. The Possibility of Miracles

I. INTRODUCTION: PLATO'S SEARCH FOR TRUTH

Plato provides the most influential case study of a person who tried to come up with his own religion through reason alone and without prior exposure to Christian thought. Under the influence of Socrates, he learned a method for establishing what we could truly know. Using geometry as the paradigm for demonstrative thinking, Plato tried to discover the meaning of the most important things in life by the same standard. Not being able to achieve that, he formulated his own mythology, not from the traditional myths of the Greeks but based on reasonable speculation. Consequently, he arrived at several hypotheses that explained how the hope required for the attainment of virtue might make sense, such as the doctrine of recollection, reincarnation, the immortality of the soul, the reality and realm of universal forms, and finally the Ultimate Form of the Good.

Plato was completely honest in admitting that though these hypotheses where adequate to count as legitimate explanations of our experience of the world, they could not be said to have been demonstrated by the standard of clear analysis that Socrates had set. However, these hypotheses were sufficiently plausible to count as live options which did some explanatory work and could not otherwise be shown to be false. Thus, Plato thought it was rational to gamble on their being true and frame one's pursuit of virtue and truth on them, since the expected gain in rationally desirable ends was greater in choosing to believe them than in suspending judgment about their truth. Just as we today may speak of the necessity of both faith and reason, Plato speaks of the need for both courage and wisdom.

Of particular note is Plato's discussion of the Ultimate Form of the Good in his book, the Republic. In this concept, Plato's speculations reach their heights while his desires are inflamed to near ecstasy. Though Plato uses the term "form" to refer to this Being, he clearly does not do so in the same sense as he uses it to talk about the universals like justice and equality. He is using it metaphorically to refer to this Being as the Ultimate Principle Being, even more real than the immutable universals, specifically because the universals still depend for their eternal existence on this self-existent Source of all varieties of reality. The closest analogy to the Good Plato can think of is the sun, because the heat and energy of the actual sun are the necessary condition of life on the earth, while the light from the sun is the necessary condition of our seeing what is in the world.

Similarly, the Good is the principle source of existence for the reality of real things and is also the source of the intellectual light by which we intellectually see the true natures of things. Also, it is the ultimate source of all goodness, since to be good for Plato is just for something to be what it is, just as a perfectly drawn square is perfect just because it is a square. Thus Plato calls it the Good. Christians cannot read this description without having their ears burn. It sounds like Plato is talking about God. It's no wonder early church theologians were so appreciative of his work.

Plato illustrates the substance and the limits of what someone might know through natural revelation with reason reflecting on its natural lights. Here we see a reasonable, if only partial, uncertain, and confused knowledge of the existence of a God-like Being , but we also see a rationale for having some answer to issues like how to be good and what will happen after death. Plato is rightly certain that there needs to be an answer but is not certain what the answer is. Although not everyone who is not a Christian believes exactly like Plato, the themes in Plato's work bear strong resemblance to themes that define other ancient and contemporary religious and philosophical traditions.

II. THINKING ABOUT THE SUN

Plato's analogy of the Sun with Ultimate Being is useful in illustrating how it is we know about God from general revelation. The sun is invisible to us not because it is in the dark but because it is too brilliant to behold. Yet we know it exists because of the role it necessarily plays in the existence and well being of life on earth. By the same token, we cannot directly see the essence of God from which to abstract the concept of God. *Finiti non capax infiniti*. The finite cannot comprehend the infinite. However, this suggests a problem. We claim that we do not know what God is yet we do know that He exists, but how is that possible? Try to answer these questions. (1) Do tigers exist? (2) Do unicorns exist? (3) Do patrengues exist? You can answer the first two questions easily but the last is hopeless to answer because you do not know what a "patrengue" is. Similarly, if we don't know what God is, how can we know if God exists?

I know that when my sink drain refuses to drain, there is a clog in my drain. I do not know what the clog is but I know that it is there. The clog is the "thing" that keeps the sink from draining. I also know that in houses which maintain a constant temperature no matter what the weather is like outside, there is a thermostat. I d not know what a thermostat really is but I know it is there. The thermostat is the "thing" that maintains the temperature in the house. While we cannot always form an idea of what something is, from direct acquaintance we can recognize the existence of things as necessary conditions for the performance of a function or the fulfilling of a role.

Looking back at our arguments for God's existence, we see that they also have this same feature about each of their conclusions. There exists a being upon which everything else depends for their existence, a being which is the uncaused first cause, a being which designed the universe, a being that is the source of thinking, intelligibility, morality, agency, and personality. In each of these cases, there is a being that does such and such a job. We argue that this is God because what people use the term "God" for is a being that does all these things.

The argument uses "God" as a name of a being rather than a word for a kind of being. But this is not at odds with the Biblical and Christian uses of "God". God is "Creator", "Redeemer", "Savior", "Father", and "Lord" – all terms that characterize something in terms of the role they realize. Based on its existence and the nature of its effects, we infer its attributes and thus produce, in certain respects, a concept of God. We know that God is necessary because the uncaused first cause cannot not exist and thus has existence as a part of its definition, unlike created things. We also know that God is one because he cannot not exist and be composed of parts since parts can be separated and bring about the cessation of the existence of the whole. We know that God does not change because he is the unchanged changer. We know that God is perfect because God must be the source of all possible degrees of perfection. We know that God must be good because the way to be not good is by the loss of some prior existing perfection. For example, sickness is not something in itself but only the absence of health. But God cannot be the ultimate cause of good and lack any prior existing perfection. And God must be personal in the sense that whatever God is, he is the source of human agency and thought. God can be more than personal but he cannot be less than personal.

I only list these as suggestions and pointers since we cannot develop the arguments here. But this indicates the kind of knowledge we have of God through natural revelation.[80]

III. EXPECTING A SPECIAL REVELATION

Granted that reason reflecting on the world leads to some knowledge of a personal God, and granting that such a God has made us to think and able to think about Him, we already grant that God permits us to know him rather than otherwise. We also

---

[80] St. Thomas Aquinas, *Summa Contra Gentiles: Book One: God*, trans. Anton C. Pegis, University of Notre Dame Press; New edition, 1991.

accept our knowledge of Him is not merely by the effort and initiative of our reason but also by the freedom of God to disclose knowledge of Him to us. In short, we know God by His own self-disclosure, by what theologians call natural revelation. We conclude that we have the necessary ingredients to make the science of theology possible; the object of study exists (God), the subject fit to take in information about the object (Humanity, divinely adapted to know God), and a medium that transmits knowledge of the object to the subject (the natural revelation of God through the world and human nature).

However, we may want to know if there is to be more than what is available from nature alone. While we think that God exists and thus that additional revelation is not impossible, we also think that God is free and need not reveal anything more about Himself. Just like in disciplines that study persons, like individual psychology, we must wait to see if the person will allow us to know anything before we can understand. And if God does make Himself known more fully, how can we be sure it is Him?

If God were to give us more knowledge of Himself, we would need some sign to us that he is doing so. It is at this point in the argument where the subject of miracles arises, since they are said to be works of God that serve as signs to his special revelation. We will take up the nature of miracles in a moment. First, we need to know if we can expect special revelation from God if we are to be motivated to go looking for it and the miracles that attest to it. Some have argued that "as the ants are to us, so are we to the gods", that is, nothing at all. For example,

Deism is the view that God exists and created the world but left it to run on its own. A Deist thinks that we should not expect special revelation or miracles since that would suggest that the creation is not good after all.

There are, however, some conditions which if true would make miracles more likely, given that God is all powerful. The first is that granting that a free God does exist, miracles are not improbable. If God did want to reveal something more to humanity, it is more likely that God would confirm it with a miracle. And if we had some evidence for a miracle that would also make it more likely that there was one. However, these conditions alone do not show a probability that there is a miracle and don't encourage us to look for one.

However, on the basis that God is good, there are features of human nature that make us more expectant of a revelation of God. If God exists, then we have the duty to worship Him. However, without a word from him, we would not know what He would be pleased to accept as our worship and our putative acts would just be presumptuous.[81] Also, we argued that humans have a constitutional pull toward ultimate meaning, which is a kind of universal hunger for God. This is natural to their being and well-being. It would be odd that a good God would create humans with a design toward ultimate meaning and then leave them to go without. Also, as Kant argues, the desire of living morally needs to be appropriately related to rationality. Living rightly must be consistent with our rational self-interest and this makes sense if

---

[81] Plato, *Euthyphro*.

there is reward and punishment after death. We should expect some disclosure about life after death to be encouraged to live morally.[82]

Further, there is the fact that when we obtain morally reflective consciousness, we are immediately aware that we have already failed morally and stand in opposition to God. We need some reconciliation but the provision for it must come from God and also be made known to us by God. We also discover that we have a pernicious tendency to return to moral failure again and again. We know that such weakness of will is not a necessary feature of being a rational agent but we also see that it is so mendacious and ubiquitous in humans that it might be called second nature. To live rightly we need help beyond ourselves, and thus we need God to show us what it could be. As J. G. Machen said, he believed in miracles because of sin. Finally, we need to make sense out of suffering, which attends everyone from cradle to grave. If God exists then there is a purpose for suffering, and a good God would help us to make sense of it.[83]

For all these reasons, we may expect an all powerful and good God to be more than likely to reveal himself with respect to these issues. The difference between the ant case and ours is the difference between ants and us. Ants are neither intelligent nor moral creatures, and function to form on their own. But humans are morally guided and meaningfully directed in virtue of being human, but are not self-sufficient in this respect. Wittgenstein

---

[82] Imannuel Kant, *Critique of Practical Reason.*
[83] J. Gresham Machen, *Christianity and Liberalism*, Wm. B. Eerdmans Publishing Company; Reprint edition, 1946.

was right: "the meaning of life is outside of life". But if a good God is there, we can expect Him to say something about it. Since we have now argued that God is there, we can expect a miracle. This does not amount to saying that there must be a miracle but only that it is rational to search for one.

By the same token, these considerations argue for the inadequacy of any religion, like Plato's, that supposes the sufficiency of what nature has to teach us about God for life and which tries to form a philosophy of life and a tradition based on that guidance. While neither depreciating what theological insights may be found in, what natural goods may be pursued by, nor the creativity used in framing devotion to such a religion, such a program will not show us how the breach with God by our transgressions may be atoned for, or how our relationship to God may be restored. It is necessarily up to God to say how we may find peace with Him.

IV. MIRACLES AND LAWS OF NATURE

But what is a miracle? We have to be careful because there are different definitions given for miracle that fail to clarify what it is or give it any foothold on experience. One definition of a miracle is "an event contrary to ordinary human experience". This is inadequate because it is too broad. It gives a necessary but not a sufficient description. On this definition, to deny a miracle would be to deny any unique event, possible or actual. There are many unique events which are unprecedented but which we would not call miraculous, such as the defeat of Napoleon at Waterloo.

Our definition for miracle is: An event which is (a) temporary, (b) an exception to the natural order of things, (c) done by the power of God, and (d) for the purpose of showing that the event is from God. Each part is important and both parts of (b) are individually important. The event must be temporary; otherwise it would be part of the natural order of things. To a theist the whole world order is the result of the action of God. A non-temporary feature of the world would not indicate a special revelation. It would also have to be an exception to the natural order of things, not just a unique event. And this assumes that there is an objective and recognizable "natural order of things". The natural laws are not merely general descriptions of typical of natural behavior, but phenomena determined by real causes in the natures of things, as we discussed in Chapter 4. If one wants to say that natural laws are just ways of describing how the world generally behaves, they could not serve to pick out a miracle because such an event would just become part of the database for generalization. The descriptions of the laws would change to accommodate the event.

Also, the event must be brought about by the power of God. For the event to be an exception from what the natural laws produce, God's power must overcome the natural course of things. Finally, a miracle is not a mere event but an action of God. As an act of God it must have an intention. Such an intention must be extraordinary as opposed to the goods provided by the natural order of things.[84]

---

[84] C. S. Lewis, *Miracles*, HarperOne, 2001.

V. OBJECTIONS TO MIRACLES FROM SCIENCE

Many have argued that no one who flips a light switch or listens to tunes on an iPod can take the possibility of miracles seriously. The success of science seems to be a reason why miracles just cannot be a live hypothesis for modern man. This seems to claim that somehow our present day mindset is superior in finding truth than any previous mindset. Yet there seems to be no basis for saying we are better than those before us at obtaining wisdom and understanding. Chronology is not a clear indication of superior reliability.

However, some say that for the scientist, miracles are unacceptable. One way to make this argument is to say that since miracles are exceptions to the laws of nature, and since the laws of nature cannot be broken, therefore miracles are impossible. However, this argument is clearly begs the question of whether miracles could have happened, since if the laws of nature were all there were, it would be true that they could not be broken. It defines miracles out of existence.

A more plausible argument does not try to argue that miracles cannot exist, but that even if they did it could not be reasonable to believe in them. Such an argument might go like this: Since miracles by definition are infrequent occurrences, and since ordinary events happen frequently and regularly, we have had much more evidence for ordinary events than we do for miracles. Since it's a principle of reasoning that we should always proportion our belief to the evidence, we are only reasonable when we believe in ordinary event and not miracles. There-fore, it is not reasonable to believe in miracles. [85]

Such an argument does not beg the question like the first, but it does seem to equivocate about what we mean by "more evidence". It is true that more evidence for a hypothesis makes it more reasonable to believe it rather than its alternatives. But having acquired a lot of evidence for the hypotheses that many events were caused by the ordinary course of natural law does not count as more evidence for the hypothesis that this specific event, said to be miraculous, was caused by the ordinary course of natural laws. Quantity of evidence does not imply relevancy of evidence. Compare this to the sighting of an Unidentified Flying Object. If twenty people claim to have never seen a UFO but one person claims they did see a UFO, the testimony of the twenty does not help us evaluate the credibility of the UFO witness. Truth is not settled by a democratic vote.

This "more evidence" argument seems to have many ridiculous implications. It seems to confuse evidence of regularity with evidence that an event is a regular event. But regularities can be evidence for singular events. For example, the regular behavior of scattered debris from an explosion helps us to identify the singularity of the Big Bang. Further such an argument would rule out singular events from being knowable such as the Pre-Cambrian explosion in the fossil record or Napoleon's loss at Waterloo. If this argument were true, it would not be reasonable for a scientist to examine singularities. But in fact, scientists are

[85] David Hume, *Dialogues Concerning Natural Religion*.

particularly interested in singular events. It would also be a research stopper for areas where we thought that we already had the natural laws down, since we could not expect anything that would differ from them. And the argument proves too much. Even if we saw a miracle, we could not be entitled to think we have experienced a miracle.

Most interestingly, this argument would make true of naturalism something that naturalism often argues against theism, namely it would make naturalism not open to falsification. We are tempted to ask what evidence the naturalist would accept to show that naturalism is false. If we present a miracle as evidence that naturalism is false, it would be rejected on the grounds that miracles are by hypothesis unique events. Since there is more evidence for regular events than for unique events, the evidence is better that there are no miracles. So it is not in principle possible to allow that there could be evidence from miracles that naturalism is false. This would succeed in insulating naturalism from refutation, which thus makes naturalism unscientific.

In chapter 4, we made the case for a science of singularities that we called "origin science". If that case is accepted, then in fact miracles can be considered scientifically respectable as a case of origin science.[86]

VI. OBJECTIONS TO MIRACLES FROM HISTORY

---

[86] R. Douglas Geivett & Gary R. Habermas eds., *In Defense of Miracles: A Comprehensive Case for God's Action in History*, IVP Academic, 1997.

Since miracles are by definition events that show God is involved, we certainly expect to find them in history if anywhere. But historians also argue that miracles are not possible objects for historical inquiry. One reason for saying this is that miracles involve God's operation which must be invisible and therefore not possibly witnessed by eyewitnesses. The problem with this is that the recognition of a miracle is a kind of inference to the best explanation. We do not reason from event to miracle and then from miracle to God. We reason from the effects of the event to God as the best explanation and thus conclude that the event was by definition a miracle. So miracles are not seen but inferred. This is not peculiar to miracles but many historical claims are about unseen causes inferred from historical records. The effects of the event are the sorts of things that do fall within the visibility of eyewitnesses and records. Also, people assume the historicity of evidence for miracles when they try to refute them.

Another charge is that history cannot tell us about miracles because history is merely subjective. History is not the study of objective facts or events but rather the exploration of various points of view. History is in the eye of the beholder and there is no privileged account of history that is distinctive for being true. On this view, all history is relative and there is no knowledge possible of the way the world was. So a history that includes miracles cannot have evidential value.

There is a subjective dimension to the writing of history. There is no point in denying that history must be written from a certain point of view. But it does not follow that since history must be told from a point of view that points of view are what history is about and nothing else. When the historical relativist says that history is merely subjective, they either intend to tell us the truth about history and thus contradict themselves by making an objective historical claim, or they are not being serious and it is just their opinion which need not bother us.

The historical relativist seems to confuse the distinction between how we discover historical facts and how we justify historical claims. I may have a hunch that my wallet is in the broom closet and look and see that it is so. But my case for showing that the wallet is in the closet is that I can see it there. The psychological reasons for how I discovered something to be the case are not the same as the reasons I give for the claim being true. Consequently, while my perspective on history is influenced deeply by my social location and upbringing, things concerning which I have had no control, what makes my construal of the historical facts legitimate is evidence apart from that perspective and is either well established or not. We charitably do not bring into account the historian's background except to explain departures from justified historical construals.

Further, several facts show that we don't take historical relativism seriously. First, we do have an established body of historical facts. Second, we have paradigm cases of good and bad history. Third, we believe that history is revisable in the light of recent discoveries. If we were relativists, what would be the point?

Another objection that historians give is that good history must be consistent with the principle of analogy, which says our past is only intelligible insofar as it resembles what we know in the present. We cannot know of cases where alchemists turn lead into gold because our contemporary experience shows that it is impossible. Since we don't have experiences of miracles today we do not reasonably expect to find them in the past. This objection turns out to be a historical version of "more evidence" argument we looked at in the case of science and has the same unattractive consequences. The analogy of the past with the present means that credible past events must conform to the present understanding of natural laws. Since a miracle is unique from the order of natural laws, it is presumed to not be an object of science and thus not an object of history. In arguing already that a miracle can be an object of science though not an ordinary event, it also is a possible object of history.

Another problem is that historical testimony is unreliable. Testimony, however, is at least generally reliable per se, and as long as the testifier is competent and has sufficient integrity with respect to the matter for which they are testifying. One does not have to be identified as a faithful, impartial, generally well-informed person to give testimony that is acceptable evidence. The same rules of evidence developed for courtroom proceedings work as well for historical evidences wherever they may apply.

Others object that trying to gather evidence is like gathering small probabilities in order to make a largely probable case. But this is false, since the aggregation of small probabilities results in even smaller probabilities. For example, the probability of rolling a six on one die is 1:6. But to roll a twelve on two dice is 1:36, even less likely. Yet the form of reasoning in history is not by aggregating probabilities but inference to the best explanation. The more details we have of a historical event, the more we can narrow the space of possible hypotheses and argue with more confidence for the best one.

A harder question is whether anyone could ever identify a historical event as a miracle. Consider the following argument. Someone infers that a particular event is a miracle. But no inference to a miracle is legitimate unless all possible naturalistic explanations are refuted. Further, no historian or scientist should consider it true that all possible naturalistic explanations have been refuted. Therefore, it is never legitimate to infer that a particular event is a miracle. If someone embraces this argument then there is no case in which they will allow that an event is a miracle.

To respond to this argument, let us consider three types of cases: (A) a person who believes that miracles can happen, (B) a person who is not a believer in miracles for reasoning like the argument above, and (C) a person who has never experienced or heard of an experience of a miracle, and has no reason to expect a miracle, but who is not necessarily closed to the idea that there could be a miracle.

Person (A), even though a believer, is not going to automatically think every event is a miracle. Even though he or she believes in God, to him or her God already is at work in the normal processes of nature according to His purposes. Further God may answer prayer without disturbing natural laws according to the ordering of providence to produce extraordinary and timely "coincidences". But God may also bring about miracles that go against the natural order. It is clear that a believer will find hard cases where they are not sure if the event is just an extraordinary event or a suspension of natural order, such as the parting of the Red Sea. But there will be for them clear cases of miracles such as turning water into wine, walking on the sea, or resurrection from the dead. A believer may become quite discerning and expert at identifying different works of God and true miracles.

Person (B) will not see any miracles at all but may encounter events that are difficult to explain naturalistically. He or she may settle for a pastiche of ad hoc explanations to cover the whole phenomenon piece by piece or simply offer a promissory note that the event in question has a naturalist explanation which we will find some day. His or her argument may be a kind of *argumentum ad ignorantum*: "It's naturalistically explained because I don't know how it could have happened otherwise." But we have allowed that it may be reasonable to tolerate some anomalous cases in a research program. Person (B) may be tempted to draw confidence from most experiences being analo ous to the present or according to natural laws, even though this is not unexpected on the hypothesis that miracles can occur.

Person (C) will not recognize any divine handiwork in the ordinary course of nature the way a believer would so these would not have any evidential value for them. But because the person remains open to evidence for a miracle, there may be some cases that may change his or her mind. In science, there are recalcitrant cases which a scientist may find too difficult to fix plausibly with ad hoc hypotheses and decide that he must actually change theories. One can imagine how difficult it may have been for Newtonian scientists to adjust to the experiments that confirmed Einstein's theory. One can further imagine a recalcitrant case where an open minded person would be willing to change his or her core metaphysical assumptions as well as his or her theories. One may decide that a systematically consistent theistic framework and the miracle inference are better than a pastiche or a promissory note.[87]

So it does not seem impossible for an open minded agnostic about miracles to identify a miracle. We conclude that history does not provide any obstacles to miracles.

VII.   CONCLUSION: AN ANSWER FOR PLATO

The existence of God and our human nature as we find it make it not improbable that He may also give us a special revelation of himself. But the goodness of God and our essential and final need for news from God for peace with God make new revelation probable and the search for them meaningful. Further, the probability of new revelation indicates the probability of a miracle done to show that it is a new revelation. So we may reasonably look for a miracle. This puts us in the position of Person (A). But even if we are agnostic about miracles, the evidence for a miracle may yet convince us if we are open to the evidence. The evidence for a miracle will be the external historical evidence, accessible through documentation of events and the internal evidence of the message testified to by the miracle and how well it seems to meet our rational expectations for it. It may

---

[87] Ibid.

be that thus the best most systematically consistent inference that can be made of historical events is that a miracle occurred, a sign of God that attests to the truth of his messenger.

The way is now clear to try to show that this actually has occurred. God has provided the world with an answer. This answer was given in the person of Jesus in history and attested to by the miracle of God raising him from the dead. Why do we think that Christianity is the way to God? Because that is what Jesus taught and God raised him from the dead. This is what we will try to show in the next two chapters.

14. The Reliability of the New Testament

I. INTRODUCTION: THE ARGUMENT

Our last chapter argued that God could and may be likely to say something to us and attest to it with a miracle even an open minded agnostic may be moved to believe. Establishing this to a plausible degree, we here claim that God had already done this in Palestine, in the person and resurrection of Jesus Christ. Since our primary sources about the life, death, and resurrection of Christ are also the defining documents for the Christian Church that is making these claims, we need to address the question of whether these documents are reliable sources of historical information. In this chapter, we will argue that the New Testament documents, that collection of writings that are taken to be sacred Scripture by the Christian tradition, are sufficiently credible historical witness to the biography of Christ.[88]

Here is our argument:

1. The burden of proof for questioning the historical reliability of any document lies with the skeptic.

---

[88] For sources that support the evidential claims made in this chapter, see: Paul Barnett, *Is the New Testament Reliable?*, *2nd ed.*, IVP Academic, 2004,

Craig Blomberg, *The Historical Reliability of the Gospels*, InterVarsity Press, 1987,

F. F. Bruce, *The New Testament Documents: Are They Reliable?*, Wm. B. Eerdmans Publishing Co., 1992,

William Lane Craig, *Reasonable Faith: Christian Truth and Apologetics*, Crossway Books; Rev Sub edition, 1994,

J. P. Moreland, *Scaling the Secular City*.

2. The skeptic has not sufficiently met the burden of proof in questioning the historical reliability of the New Testament.

3. Therefore, the New Testament ought to be received as a reliable witness to history.

This argument here is not that the New Testament is to be treated like a single authority, nor does it necessarily apply with equal strength to each of the documents or parts of documents in the New Testament. What we offer is the consideration that historical credibility attaches sufficiently well to enough of the New Testament that a reliable and interesting account of Christ's biography can be reconstructed. It is not possible for us here to explore all the details of this, but we will try to present enough to give some idea of the credibility of the New Testament.

In defense of premise (1), we argue for a *prima faci*e assumption of its truth on the basis of the irrationality of making a practice of deceiving others. The argument is famously associated with Immanuel Kant. Affirming that something is the case to another person presupposes trusting in affirmations made to the one doing the affirming. We can imagine that affirmations between persons are arranged like dominoes, each standing up next to the other assured that it also will stand up. But if any affirmation proves false, all the others fail as well like falling dominoes. This illustrates that society cannot function in a situation were lying is accepted. So, generally speaking, we do not expect to get far based on a practical acceptation of lying, including lying in a document. For that reason we should give the benefit of the doubt to documents unless proven guilty of deceit.

Furthermore, our standard of confidence, as we mentioned before, is the same as a court of law where the burden is similarly placed on proving the lack of credibility of a document or witness. Many of the relevant documents that discuss Jesus are in the form of personal and circular letters addressed to local congregations and which address their specific conditions. Such mail would be taken to be *prima facie* credible in a court of law. So we take it that the New Testament is reliable unless proven otherwise.

Our main burden then will be to show that (2) is true.

II.   GENERAL PRINCIPLES OF RELIABILTY

There are three general tests for evaluating the credibility of the New Testament documents; (a) the internal test, (b) the external test, and (c) the bibliographical test. There is much that could be said, but we will only pass over each one here.

The internal test asks whether or not there is internal coherence in the text itself. Is the content of the text internally consistent or does it betray itself in any way as a fabrication or a falsehood. While each of the New Testament documents do not merely tell a history or record a list of facts, they consistently express the intention to tell the truth. The differences between the accounts actually help with their credibility. If they squared with each other in every way including using the same language in each case, the four of them would appear like a story that was conspired beforehand. What we have is a diversity of perspectives, languages, and details, indicating diverse viewpoints on the same subject matter. The internal evidence of the text speaks against the possibility of a late accumulation of tales developed for use in various dispersed congregations and instead points to a common body of facts.[89]

The external test asks whether the document fits with what we know from other sources about the time and place. We are not going to develop this here but invite you to search and see for yourself. It is not only the case that many past Palestinian and Mediterranean archeological discoveries have confirmed the historicity of the New Testament stories (like the discovery of rolling stone covered tombs, the pool of Sidon, the James' ossuary) but that discoveries made practically every year confirm this. Search and see.[90]

The final test is the bibliographic test. This asks how well attested is the manuscript evidence for a document. We do not possess any of the original documents on many of the great works of the ancient past, such as Plato's dialogues or the works of the great Roman orators. We typically have only a few (1 – 10 or so) copies, many of which appear hundreds of years later than the originals (around 800 – 1000 CE). These are accepted as authoritative guides to reconstructing the original work. If that is sufficient for the acceptance of these works, then how much more acceptable must be the New Testament, of which of which we have over 5000 pieces of manuscript evidence, some of which is

---

[89] F. F. Bruce, *New Testament History*, Galilee / Doubleday, 1983.
[90] John McRay, *Archeology and the New Testament*, Baker Academic, 2008.

as close as a 100 years from the original events. We even have some quotes from the New Testament carved in stone. One can imagine as important to the church as the New Testament would be, assuming that it is the history and tradition given by the Apostles, that there would be extensive copying with great attention to detail to try to get the copies right. The evidence fails to disconfirm this and even makes it probably the case.

The fact that we do not have the original manuscripts from those authors' hands does not mean that we do not have the resources to reasonably reconstruct the text, especially from so much manuscript evidence. Even if the original instance of the text in the original document is lost, we can discern the text in its later instances in the manuscript evidence, just as we can recognize that modern paperbacks have the same text of Dickens's *A Tale of Two Cities* as on the paper it was first written. This process of comparing and evaluating the evidence for the most likely reconstruction of the text is called text criticism. Through it, even though there remain a few discrepancies, none of the essential doctrines of Christianity are lost or affected. Many other doctrines also remain clear besides the essential ones. Most significantly, this includes the doctrine of the inspiration of Scripture, which will be important to know for chapter 16.

So we conclude that when it comes to the basic tests for reliability, the New Testament satisfies them to a more than substantial degree.

III.   SKEPTICISM OF RELIABILITY

John G. Hartung

However, skeptics of the reliability of the New Testament documents offer grounds for dismissing the *prima facie* case for it. They believe it reasonable to question the prior likelihood that the early church would want to preserve a collection of historically reliable documents. Several such reasons offered include:

a. There was no special value placed on history by the people of the first century. Historical accuracy is a modern value not an ancient one.

b. From the account itself, there is no documentation of the actual life of Christ by the disciples that could pass beyond to the future. There are no stories of the disciples or anyone else taking notes or functioning like secretaries during their personal time with Christ.

c. The authors of the New Testament had a very strong ideology. It is expected that ideology affects the telling of history to favor the ideologist.

d. Most specifically, the New Testament church had no interest in the actual history of Jesus precisely because they thought they had the words of the living Christ communicated to them through church prophets. They were celebrating the risen living Christ in the present so there was nothing worth noting about the pre-risen Jesus. Consequently, we have good reason, says the skeptic, not to expect historically reliable information about the life of Jesus from the New Testament.

IV. THE ERROR THEORY: FORM CRITICISM

Still, if the New Testament is unreliable, why is there a widely held perception in the church that it is? It is not enough for the skeptic to offer grounds for skepticism without also explaining how it is that such skepticism is not recognized. In normal cases, such deception only affects the few, so why are so many deceived?

An explanation offered for why so many are systematically mistaken about something is called an *error theory*. In the case of New Testament reliability, the error theory is provided by the so-called higher criticism of the New Testament, particularly in form criticism. According to form criticism, the New Testament consists of particular units of text that have a highly specific structure, such as hymns, creeds, stories, and parables. Some form critics would also add myths, legends, and sagas. The presence of structuring is explained by having a specific purpose for framing the text in that form. So it is suggested that these various units of text were created to meet felt needs in the local churches for liturgy, conduct training, or pastoral care. For example, they claim that the stories of Jesus raising children from the dead were written to encourage families that had lost children during the days of the church. The aggregation of these stories into the Gospels creates the impression of a life of Jesus that in fact is just a kind of wisdom literature. But this explains the appearance of a history of Jesus that is not historical.

V. REBUTAL TO THE ERROR THEORY

In response to the error theory, there is no need to deny the important observation that various portions of New Testament material seems to be shaped for specific purposes. There are certainly cases of parables, creeds, hymns, and the like that are clear instances of formalization. However, the story offered by form criticism is implausible for the following reasons.

First, there's no good reason to deny that the forms of New Testament text were given to it by the original authors. This is especially plausible concerning Jesus' parables, given the analogies between Jesus' method of teaching and other rabbis, who prepared their lessons in order to be memorized and preserved by their students. Also, the portions of text in the Gospels contain what I will call "Jesus-isms" which are both peculiar to him and his setting, such as "Amen, Amen", "Abba" for referring to God, phrases like "How much more . . ." and so on. These were attributed to Jesus in the Gospels but were no longer used by others in the early church. Therefore these "Jesus-isms" would not play a role in forms of text designed to meet the needs of the church that came after Jesus. The form critical approach does not expect them.

Many stories told in the Gospel accounts deal with concerns that were no longer relevant to the early church, such as the conflict with the Pharisees and the special favor Jesus shows toward Israel. Also, concerns that were relevant to the early church such as spiritual gifts, the inclusion of the Gentiles, circumcision, the relation of church and state are not dealt with at all in the Gospels. The gospels contain many things that arguably would be counterproductive in the early church such as embarrassing stories about the disciples, now apostles and leaders, such as James and John asking who is the greatest or Peter's denial of Jesus. Also, there are inconvenient things said by Jesus about divorce and fasting and the criminal death of Jesus on the cross. Also, Paul could have won more authority for his distinctive teachings if he put them in the mouth of Jesus.

Too much material is inconvenient for the project of tailoring text to fit current needs. It's inconvenient in ways that suggest a willingness to present material come what may. As we said, the unity of material suggests a common tradition of facts underlying the Gospels. This would not be plausible if they were the gathering of diverse units adapted merely to local needs. The form critical theory of the text is not adequate to the phenomena and thus fails to succeed as an error theory.

VI. THE UNREASONABLENESS OF SKEPTICISM

There are also things to be said against the proposed grounds for skepticism. Against (a), while ancient authors did not have the standards and methods of contemporary historical research, there are clear examples of ancient historiography around and before the first century that demonstrate that people did understand and care about the distinction between true history and false history. Both the Greeks and the Romans had a literary tradition of history writing for posterity and their writing was the model for the work of the distinguished Jewish historian, Josephus. In particular, the Gospels resemble the genre of literature of hero biography that was well used at the time. Such biographies were more than history, encouraging the reader to model their lives on the hero, but this did not detract from the historical truth. The details given about the life of the hero were meant to show that the hero was no mere moral fiction. Historicity was essential to the authority of the story. The New Testament indicates in several places, most notably at the beginning of Luke's gospel, that it intends to present a true researched record of the life of Jesus.

Against (b), even though there may not have been any secretaries or reporters as such among the disciples, this would not have been either necessary or desired as the most reliable means of transmitting material. Studies in the works of rabbis in the second century show that they had skills to assure the transmission of material orally through careful memorization techniques. Some rabbis were known to have the entire Old Testament memorized. There is no reason to think that the methods in 200 AD were any different from the traditional methods observed for centuries. One can see the need for them in what was mainly an oral culture. While Jesus was certainly a lot more than a rabbi, there is no reason to think he was less of one in respect to teaching methods. The shaping of texts into parables and prayers is in part to facilitate memorization. It would not be surprising that this came from Jesus himself. Further, there is greater agreement amongst the sayings of Jesus than the stories of his deeds, just as we would expect from an orally preserved tradition.[91]

---

[91] Richard Baukham, *Jesus and the Eyewitnesses: The Gospels as Eyewitness Testimony*, Wm. B. Eerdmans, 2006.

Against (c), while it is true that often ideology can lead to the distortion of information, it is not always so. In fact, ideology can be a powerful motivation for accuracy of information. Contrary to the skeptic, it is difficult to imagine that the early church would not be interested in as many specifics about the life of Jesus as possible, and that they would want to present those facts as carefully as possible, given that Jesus was crucified on a cross as a common criminal. People would say, "If Jesus is so good, why did they execute him?" The presumption of guilt would need to be dismissed.

Finally, against (d), there is no evidence that the early church was receiving continual messages from the risen Christ charismatically through church prophets. We see evidence of this sort of thing in Gnostic and other non-orthodox literature but not in the New Testament sources. The one place we do see Jesus giving prophecy in the New Testament is in the Book of Revelation, but here it is clear that he is not giving information about the days and sayings of his earthly life, but about the future. In the book of Acts, however, we see details of the life of Christ being given in the sermons preached by the early church. The experience of the Risen Christ, whatever that was, in the early church was not the sort of thing to create disinterest in the life of Jesus but rather the proclamation of it.

VII.   THE EVIDENCE FOR RELIABILITY

So having responded to these skeptical concerns, we are back to the *prima facie* case of the tests of reliability. It is worthwhile to see that scholarship in the area of New Testament related studies has not diminished but rather strengthened the case for confidence in the historicity of the New Testament.

Even unbelieving scholars generally place the date of the original writing of the various New Testament documents before 100 CE. Jesus died c. 33 CE. The typical length of time for legendary stories to develop about a historical figure is at least two generations. Even with these dates, there still had not been enough time. Yet even many skeptically and critically inclined scholars would date the texts earlier. John A.T. Robinson, notorious for the accommodating work "Honest to God", was compelled to date all the New Testament books as being written before 70 CE when the city of Jerusalem fell to the Roman Army.[92]

Not all of Paul's letters are recognized as his by all scholars but seven of them are. Paul's letters are thought to be the earliest written of the NT documents at 48 CE, less than 20 years after the death of Christ. There is clearly no time for legends to develop. But Paul already has a high view of Christ as Lord and Savior and Son of God. Also, there is no evidence of any evolution or change in Paul's doctrine of Christ from one letter to the next. Paul's Christology was received in complete from the beginning of his ministry. Further, Paul's account of his visit with the other apostles in Galatians 1 and 2 shows that they approved of his Christology. This suggests that their doctrine also was a high Christology that pre-dates Paul's. Paul uses

---

[92] John A. T. Robinson, *Redating the New Testament*, Wipf & Stock Publishers, 2001.

hymns and creeds that were already in use in the early church which also reflect a high Christology. Especially noteworthy is the formula at the beginning of 1 Corinthians 15. These all reflect views of the church before Paul.

The Synoptic Gospels (Matthew, Mark, and Luke) typically receive a date after 70 CE. The main reason for this is that all three predict the fall of Jerusalem, which happened in 70 CE. The assumption is that they so faithfully detail what happened that they must have already known about it. Of course, this assumes that predictive prophecy is impossible. For someone open to predictive prophecy, they might allow for an earlier date. Scholars hold that the internal evidence between these Gospels indicates that Mark was written first, since both Matthew and Luke draw upon him. Mark's style and language most closely resembles the style and language of both 1 Peter and Peter's sermons in Acts, which fits the tradition that he was the secretary for the Apostle Peter. Another source besides Mark seems to have been used by Matthew and Luke for many of the sayings of Jesus, traditionally called "Q" from the German word 'quelle" which means 'source'. This source may have been a written document of the orally transmitted saying of Jesus, but there is no manuscript evidence for it. This would make sense if Jesus used rabbinical techniques of oral transmission to preserve his sayings.

Luke also wrote the Acts of the Apostles which by internal evidence should be dated after the three Synoptic Gospels. But the date of Acts should be about 61-64 AD. There are several reasons for this; Acts has no mention of the war of the Jews against Rome or the fall of Jerusalem. It does not mention the deaths of the Apostles that appear in its pages or of the Nero's persecution of the Christians. It deals with issues that took place earlier in history, such as the circumcision debate, and the Gentile issue but leaves Paul in Rome for the first time awaiting trial. And it does not elaborate on the significant Jewish customs which would be alien to Greek speakers that dominate over the church in the 50's CE. But if Acts has an earlier date, so then must the synoptic Gospels. It seems the only reason for dating them later is the presupposition against prophecy.[93]

One critical group of scholars, the Jesus Seminar, set a rule that only sayings attributed to Jesus that were not also found in either Jewish environment or used by the early church would be considered as authentically his.[94] This rule seems most unreasonable and bound to generate too many false negatives. But even applying this rule, it turns out that the remaining sentences still exhibit a high doctrine of Christ. Albert Schweitzer in his own critical work earlier also could only conclude that the high Christology was coming from Jesus himself.[95]

Finally, the sermons in the first 12 chapters in Acts, these represent the earliest formulations of the thought of the church before the Synoptic recordings. The language indicates a more primitive time before the developments that came with the Gentile missions. The Christology is the closest formulation in

---

[93] J. P. Moreland, *Scaling the Secular City.*

[94] Robert Walker Funk and the Jesus Seminar, *The Gospel of Jesus: According to the Jesus Seminar*, Polebridge Press, 1999.

[95] Albert Schweitzer, *The Quest for the Historical Jesus*, trans, W. Montgomery, Dover Publications, 2005

time to Christ himself and also reflects many of the same themes of a high view of Christ and his work on the cross. The detail included that the Apostles began to preach seven weeks after the crucifixion lends credibility to the account since there seems to be no motive for saying this.

So many strands of internal evidence seem to show that the original sources of the New Testament witness can be traced back to the time immediately following the events of which they speak. At this point, the focus and activity of the Apostles and the early church was in and around the vicinity of Jerusalem and Israel. There was plenty of opportunity for counter-witnesses to the apostolic account to come forward and contradict their reports. They could have taken a ship and started to preach anywhere else in the Roman Empire if they wanted to avoid that. But it is clear that they did not nor were they afraid of being called on their facts in Jerusalem. And no one could be received as an Apostle unless they witnessed the resurrected Christ. Finally, they experienced the great danger of being killed for what they were saying and had motivation to keep silent about it. That they did not run or hide or keep silent lends credibility to their testimony.

VIII. CONCLUSION: UNREASONABLE DOUBT

In conclusion, there are no historically based reasons to doubt the witness of the apostles to Jesus and his life, death, and resurrection. A believer in the New Testament witness cannot be accused of being closed minded to actual history. The only reason for disbelief could be philosophical presuppositions that rule out miracles and prophecy. But our arguments for God and our preliminary discussion about miracles challenge those presuppositions. Consequently, we dismiss the case against (2) above and hold the argument to be sound.

Notice that in defending the historical character of the New Testament, we did not appeal to it as the inspired, infallible Word of God. We avoided the question begging argument, "We believe that the New Testament is reliable because it's the Word of God. We believe the New Testament is the Word of God because it says it's the Word of God. We believe what the New Testament says because it's reliable." We have modestly and tactically made the case that whether the New Testament is the Word of God or not, it is at least historically reliable and a competent witness to the events it reports. In our next discussion, we will examine what it reports about Christ's Teaching and his Resurrection.

15. When Truth Became Flesh

I. INTRODUCTION: JESUS HIMSELF

Let us take stock of where we are. Having argued that it is possible to defend miracles for open minded agnostics, we then asked whether we might find any such in history. Our answer is that there was at least one miracle case in Palestine during the days of Jesus. We then argued that we have sources about events at that time that are historically reliable, namely the New Testament Documents. Having argued for this claim, we will take it as established. Our next task is to see what the New Testament reports and see if it provides evidence for a miracle.

But it is also important that we remember what we argued a miracle might be for, namely as a sign that God is providing a special revelation of Himself to his intelligent creatures, for reasons such as the ones suggested in our discussion of miracles in Chapter 12. We will argue that the New Testament shows that Jesus had an exceptional nature and purpose and that his resurrection is the miracle by which God gave His imprimatur on Jesus and his message. First, we shall look at an argument that Jesus is who he says he was and we will look at the resurrection evidence.

The objection is often raised that, even if the New Testament sources were reliable, the church had misconstrued what these sources say about Jesus' view of himself. However, there is plenty of evidence to support that the concept of Jesus held in the early church was traceable to Jesus.

1. Jesus says over and over again in his ministry "Verily, Verily, I say unto you that . . .". It is clear from the context that this formula functions in place of the use of "Thus says the Lord" in the mouths of the prophets. This is illustrated in the example of the Sermon on the Mount,[96] "You have heard it said . . . But I say . . ." The import of this to the crowd is that they see Jesus as teaching with authority and not as the scribes, that is, that his style of teaching was making a bold and extraordinary claim about his regard of himself.

2. Jesus says of himself to the Pharisees, "Before Abraham was, I am", not as you might expect "Before Abraham was, I was". Jesus is affirming a pre-existence, but more than that, he uses the formula "I am" to refer to himself -- a formula which is the same form as the covenant name God gives Himself in the Torah[97] something the import of which the Pharisees would likely see immediately. In fact, the Pharisees in the Synoptics are quicker to see the divine claims of Jesus than the apostles.

3. When Jesus asks the disciples "Who do you say that I am?", Peter says "You are the Christ, the Son of the Living God". Jesus responds by saying "No man has revealed this to you, but only the Father in heaven". He claims that Peter's claim ("Son of the living God") about him is the result of divine revelation and thus cannot be considered false.

---

[96] Matthew 5-7.
[97] Exodus 6.

4. Jesus refers to God in prayer as "Abba". Although the Jews agreed that God was rightly considered their Father, they would never have used "Abba" to address God because it would be seen as grossly inappropriate. In a sentimental mood, we often say that Abba means "daddy" but we are getting caught up in the endearing feel of the expression. More than this, "Abba" is an honorific that can only be used by people in certain relationships. Compare with Japanese honorifics. In Japanese, suffixes are used with names to indicate social order and relative standing. So Tanaka-san means "Mr. Tanaka", Tanaka-sama means "Lord Tanaka", Tanaka-kun means "my peer Tanaka", and Tanaka-chan means "My dear Tanaka" or "My child Tanaka". Similarly, "Abba" can only be properly used by someone who is actually the child of the father in question and the Jews would never have used it to address God. The precise implication would be that they were progenies direct of God or adopted into God's personal family which was not regarded as being the case by the Jews. Such a claim would be presumption of the highest order and unacceptable to them. But Jesus used it when addressing God.

5. Jesus responds to the statement by the high priest "Are you the son of God?" with "Thou hast said". Many have taken this to mean "That's what you say (and not necessarily me)". But the high priest must be accorded respect in court. Jesus responds to the court as a legitimate court and sees his testimony as testimony. Thus, he is forbidden by the commandment "Thou shall not give false testimony" to say anything false. So when he spoke it was to answer the questions truthfully. The remark is a formula that asserts that "It is exactly as you have said it." The

response by the high priest, "What further need have we of witnesses?" indicates that Jesus' remark amounts to a confession.[98]

6. Finally, he used as his preferred self-designation "Son of Man" throughout his ministry. The term could mean several things to anyone with an Old Testament background, but toward the end of his ministry he made clear that the sense he had in mind was the Heavenly Divine Figure referred to in Daniel 7. So there is ample evidence in the text to support that Jesus saw himself as peculiarly identified with the God of Israel.

There are four distinct frameworks we need to consider when we think of Jesus and his claims; the literary-historical framework, the philosophical- theological framework, the psychological framework, and the moral framework. The historical framework asks whether the literary accounts about Jesus contain historically reliable information about Him. This we already argued in the previous chapter, but let us also add that when it comes to the specifics about Jesus' life as written in the Gospels and the speeches in Acts, we find that there is a great deal of unity about the life, death, and burial of Jesus and a great deal of diversity about the resurrection appearances – which is just what we would expect given the nature of the purported events. Further, while harmonization of the Gospel accounts of Jesus' life is possible, it is not easy. But this lends credibility to their witness since on the one hand their testimonies do not ultimately contradict each other, but on the other there is no

---

[98] Matthew 26, Mark 14.

evidence of a conspiracy of agreeing about what to say beforehand. The diversity of writing suggests authentic witnesses from different perspectives.

Many external sources and archeological finds confirm the events within the New Testament, as we mentioned before. Further, the New Testament materials make committed assertions on too many particulars that seem to be not germane to the story and which would make it vulnerable to contradiction to suggest contrivance after the fact, such as the detials surrounding Jesus' life in Capernaum, the feeding of the 5,000, the denials of Peter. These accounts are in blatant contrast to much later apocryphal literature in being free of fabulisms, such as talking crosses, angelic parades, and so on, and in being more natural and prosaic, which attest to its proximity to the events. There was no time for legendary wonders to develop. Further, if we assume with critics that the New Testament is myth, legend, and saga, we should expect to find a prior and related factual account of Jesus that the legends build on and depart from. But there is no evidence that such a background exists. We take it then that there really was a Jesus Christ and that the New Testament is a reliable source of some information about him. Jesus is not a legend.[99]

From the philosophical-theological framework, we ask whether Jesus' self-concept was consistent with itself and logically possible and whether it was inconsistent with the background in the Old Testament, since Jesus claims to fulfill that

---

[99] Craig A. Evans, *Fabricating Jesus: How Modern Scholars Distort the Gospels*, IVP Books, 2008. See also the references from Footnote 1 in chapter 14.

account. We have to be careful because, by the nature of the claim, we have to admit that there are many aspects that are unfathomable to us being finite and morally fragile, but it should not be the case that there are any explicit contradictions in the account that would make Jesus' nature heretical or logically impossible. The claims Jesus makes about himself are *prima facie* implausible and shocking, something of which Jesus seems aware. We need to dispel any logical grounds for such implausibility.

How can someone be both God and man at the same time? God is timeless but man is time bound? God is unchanging, but man is changeable. And so on. The charge is that conceiving of God and man as co-instantiating in one person leads to affirming and denying the same attribution to the same subject. This would be like saying there could be a square circle, which is incoherent. Thus, we could not logically accept the claim that Jesus is God.

This charge is certainly significant and we will not be able to do it justice in a short space. However, we can suggest a basic strategy. Consider:

> Garfield is a cat.
> Garfield is warm-blooded.
> Garfield is striped.

To say that Garfield is a cat is to say what kind of thing Garfield is. "Cat" is a term referring to a kind that something could be. To say that Garfield is warm-blooded is to refer to a feature that Garfield necessarily must have in order to be the kind of thing he is – a cat, since cats are mammals. But to refer to Garfield being striped is to refer to a feature that Garfield does have but does not need to have in order to be the kind of thing he is. That is to say, Garfield is striped but he does not need to be striped to be a cat. However, Garfield cannot be a cat without being warm-blooded.

The question is whether the idea of one person jointly having two natures, or being of two distinct kinds, is conceivable, and if what is essential to one nature is contingently possible for the other and vice versa. For example, the same person can be both a mathematician and a bicyclist since, while being good at math is essential to be a mathematician but not essential to be a bicyclist, and while having legs is essential to being a bicyclist but not essential to being a mathematician, it is possible without risking a contradiction for a mathematician to have legs and for a bicyclist to be good at math. This is true of all the essential attributes of each. They all can be possible attributes for the other so that one can coherently be both.

Similarly, if for the sake of addressing this issue we take "God" as a kind, then there are certain qualities something must have if it is God, and others it may have but need not have to be God. Also, taking man as a kind, there are certain features something must have if it is a man and other features it may have but need not have in order to be a man. What the incarnation claim asserts then is that Jesus is one person who is both God and Man, that being God does not require being man to be God but may allow being man, and that man does not require being God to be man but may allow being God. If this is logically possible then it is not incoherent for the same person to be God and man.

This is the basic idea but it has to be tested against each possible set of apparently contradictory features. We will only use two examples to illustrate. First, God is eternal and man is not, so how can the same person be both eternal and not eternal. If we think of man's mortality as meaning that he will necessarily die, and if this means that death is the end of existence for man, then of course, there is no way to avoid a contradiction. But the Christian view of death is not as the end of existence but as a dramatic change in existence to a new form of it. To be eternal is to always exist and men are creatures that have at one time not existed. However, it is not essential to human nature as such that it one time did not exist. It is conceivable that a human being eternally exist as a being held in existence by an act of God. Such a being would still be human but not one that did not exist at a time. So always existing is not something that must be true of something if it is human, but it may be the case for a human, like being striped in the case of Garfield being a cat. Second, humans must face death, the suffering of the experience of going from one kind of life to another. God does not require that experience to be God, but God may undergo that experience and still be God, especially since death is not the cessation of existence. It may be a surprise to think of God that way, but it is not incoherent. Thus, Jesus can be eternal and face death.

Even these examples are going to raise other questions, which may have many different sources for the resolution of apparent contradictions, and which will have surprising consequences of our view of God and man. I cannot say this is merely left as an exercise for the reader, because this definitely involves some intellectual heavy lifting. Suffice to say that this is left as an exercise to the would-be budding theologian. At any rate, we claim that a critical mass of resolutions to such apparent contradictions is available to reflective thinkers sufficient to render plausible the claim that the conclusion is not incoherent. Search and see.[100]

As for the consistency of the incarnation claim against the Old Testament background, a Biblical theological study of the Old Testament points to the juxtaposition of a promised leadership who belongs to the line of David, but also to the fallibility and inadequacy of merely human leadership. This is developed in the Old Testament writing prophets. While we cannot explore this theme adequately here, we point out that the following passages of the Old Testament seem to anticipate the coming of God as a man; Psalm 110:1-7, Isaiah 9:6, Micah 5:2, and Zechariah 12:8-10.[101]

II. LORD, LIAR, OR LUNATIC

With respect to the psychological framework, the question is whether Jesus is psychologically properly functioning and mature when he claims to be God. For example, while granting that we do have reliable accounts, Albert Schweitzer felt com-

---

[100] Thomas V. Morris, *The Logic of God Incarnate*, Wipf & Stock Publishers, 2001.
[101] Michael L. Brown, *The Real Kosher Jesus: Revealing the Mysteries of the Hidden Messiah*, Frontline, 2012.

pelled to conclude that Jesus had lost his mind in the sense of being much like a mad, apocalyptic end of the world preacher.

As we have seen, it is clear that many of the things Jesus said indicated subtly but clearly that he saw himself in a unique and privileged relation to God. In a normal case, we would think of someone who claimed that he was virtually God as insane, but Jesus' behavior and the reactions of others toward him indicate an optimally functioning personality rather than an improperly functioning one. Normally, in the presence of someone who was suffering from insanity or any other dysfunction or disorder, we would inevitably feel superior to them; "There but for the grace of God go I". But no one felt that way about Jesus. In fact, the reaction of people toward him was just the opposite. People from all classes were humbled and intimidated by him. Furthermore, there is evidence in the accounts that Jesus often knew people better than they knew themselves, indicating social alertness. But Jesus did not necessarily charm people. He often confronted them with ingenious responses.

It is difficult to regard Jesus as being mad, given his behavior and conversation. Jesus displayed great flourishes of insight and brilliance which was evident to his contemporaries. He was able to answer the Pharisees and the Sadducees when they tried to trap him in various ways. He was able to impress the Roman authorities, particularly Pilate. Even though he claimed to be God, his presentation of himself was vastly different from the others who claimed to be the Messiah to gain a political following. The circumlocutory method he used to convince the disciples of his deity was designed not to draw attention to himself but to allow time for them to recognize him as God, a goal he expected them not to realize until after he died. Jesus had two main claims that he wanted to assert, both of which were completely unacceptable to the Jews and the disciples; (a) that he was the Son of God and (b) that he was to die on the cross. Jesus' careful way of handling these claims illustrates to a great depth his competence in accomplishing goals. It does not seem plausible to think of Jesus as psychologically lacking, compared to paradigmatically normal cases.

The final framework is the moral, in which we ask whether we can expect Jesus to act with integrity and character, or think that in making his claims he was deliberately misleading people for malicious ends. However, Jesus and his distinctive teachings make us want to rank him with Gandhi, Martin Luther King, or Mother Theresa in terms of what he expected from his followers. And further, his miracles, while being tied directly to his message, also had an essential element of ministry. The miracles such as healings, exorcism, feeding, and so on that he performed clearly regarded the good of whomever they were performed on. Jesus did not perform miracles designed to satisfy mere curiosity or to impress the greats of his time. Most importantly, Jesus was willing to die for the good of others. Given the way he described the meaning of the cross, and given that the profit of going to the cross for any self-centered gain is absent, the character of Christ is manifest.

Further, it is difficult to see what selfish motive he could have had. We must presume that in choosing to risk his life to present himself as one with God, it would have to promise a sufficiently large return on the deed within a reasonable time frame. But given the cultural circumstances, there is nothing that Jesus could reasonably expect but that his teaching and behavior would lead to his death. So what would an intelligent but malevolent person hope to gain? Furthermore, the Gospels provide ample evidence that suggests that the character of Jesus was exemplary, more so than the characters that surrounded him. He had an authority that was in part due to his integrity and freedom from hypocrisy.[102]

Here is a story that ties this all together. When I was in graduate school, the Law school at my university sponsored a guest lecture by a legal professor who wanted to argue that the Jewish leaders were justified in arranging to have Jesus killed. His argument turned on the distinction that he took special care to make clear between the moral law and the positive law. The moral law recognizes those universal and objective principles of good conduct and general equity. The positive law is a set of prescriptions made in view to applying the moral law but which are stipulated by a competent authority and could have been otherwise. An example of a positive law is the law that everyone in America must drive on the right side of the road. It is an arbitrary matter whether one drives on the left or right side of the road. But it is necessary to have an enforced consensus on which

---

[102] Craig, *Reasonable Faith*,
C. S. Lewis, *Mere Christianity*, HarperSanFrancisco; Revised & Enlarged edition, 2001,
Josh McDowell, *More Than a Carpenter*, Living Books, 1987.
Moreland, *Scaling the Secular City*.

side everyone should drive on so that all may drive safely. Other countries accomplish the same thing by requiring their citizens to drive on the left side. So while a positive law is arbitrary in itself, the law is important. The authority for positive law is the authority of the state which decides what the positive law is.

It is clear that the distinction between moral and positive law applies to the Old Testament Law. There the moral law is distinguished from both the civil and the ceremonial law. While statutes of ceremony and society have to conform to principles of general equity expressed in part by the Ten Commandments, many also stipulate certain procedures which could have been otherwise, such as observing the Sabbath on the seventh day rather than the first day of the week. So it was relevant for the speaker to appeal to this distinction, given the Old Testament background Jesus shared with his opponents.

This allowed the speaker to make his point. He conceded that Jesus was widely recognized as having followed the moral law perfectly. But his complaint was that Jesus flouted the positive law. In doing this, Jesus was an ingenious provocateur, knowing that such behavior would only offend the Jews and no one else. According to this view, Jesus in spite of perfectly keeping the moral law was a bad man. To illustrate his case, the professor introduced into evidence the account in the Gospels of the healing of the paralytic.[103] Jesus has the paralytic walk while carrying a load on the Sabbath in front of the leaders. Though his healing service to the paralytic was paradigmatically in keeping

---

[103] Luke 5.17-26.

with the moral law to love one's neighbor, his breaking the Sabbath by carrying a load was designed to get the goat of the Pharisees. Thus they had a right to vindicate themselves and see to it that Jesus was killed. So the professor claimed that while Jesus followed the moral law, he deliberately broke the positive law as an offensive act against the Pharisees.

During the question and answer time, I remarked how surprised I was that he had chosen that story to support his view, after making such a clear distinct between moral and positive law, since it seemed precisely the point that Jesus was making under the circumstances. I asked him, "Who would have sufficient authority to change the positive law?" His smile went away and he said, "The Messiah of God". After Jesus tells the victim "Your sins are forgiven", the Pharisees complain, "Who can forgive sins but God alone?" Jesus showed that he does have that authority to forgive sins by showing that he has the authority to do miracles, as his preface "Which is easier to do . . ." makes clear. So the professor realized that his point was question-begging in light of his own evidence. This case illustrates how Jesus had a unique view of his own self but could not be accused on that occasion of being immoral or malfunctioning. Jesus defends his right to claim authority over the determination of positive law and carries out the moral law by healing the paralytic with a miracle.

This leads us to this familiar argument: (1) Either Jesus is God or a bad person. (2) Jesus is not a bad person. (3) Therefore, Jesus is God. The conclusion is valid and the premises are reasonable given the New Testament evidence. If a person is a good person, both moral and sane, then if he asserts anything, it must be true in his own judgment and his judgment must be competent. But Jesus asserts that he is one with God, as we have argued from the historical New Testament evidence. If he is a good man then he is telling the truth that he is God. But if he is not God, then he is not telling the truth either because he cannot and was thus not sane or competent, or because he will not and so was a bad person. So (1) is true. But we have argued that the evidence does not support that he was either incompetent or immoral, so (2) is true. So, we may conclude reasonably that (3) is true.

While the argument is a valid deduction, the premises are not logical truths. A deductive argument is only as strong as its weakest premise. Premise (2) is the premise most subject to the exigencies of evidence. However, if the historical testimony of the New Testament is accepted, the evidence it provides makes the thesis that Jesus was other than substantially moral or optimally functional very unreasonable. We may affirm Jesus as a truthful person with a moral certainty.

Confidence in this simple argument is how well it has stood the test of time. One may think of the various quests for "Historical Jesus", including the recent Jesus Seminar as specific attempts by various coteries of liberal scholars to find a way out of this argument. Each one has gone exhausted without finding a commonly accepted satisfactory way to do so.[104]

---

[104] Ben Withirington III, *The Jesus Quest: The Third Search for the Jew of Nazareth*, IVP Academic; 2nd edition, 1997.

Some take the view that Jesus was a creative religious genius and adopted a view of himself such as you might find in Asia, seeing himself as God in the same way all things are all ultimately God in pantheism, or seeing himself as manifestation of God on earth as an avatar or a bodhisattva. But if this were so, he would likely have been marginalized in the strongly monotheistic community of Israel. It is unlikely that anyone in first century Palestine would have developed such a view in that context.

III. THE SLAUGHTER OF THE CHRIST: DEATH

Turning from Jesus' account of himself to the subject of his resurrection, we recall what we learned about miracles, namely that the possibility of identifying a miracle is based on facts that in themselves prove accessible to historical investigation, just as facts that are uniform with our regular experience, but which provide evidence that miraculous intervention could be the best explanation for them. In this case, we will look at four facts that are accessible to us and for which there seems no better explanation but the miracle of the resurrection. Again our historical source for these facts is the New Testament, the historicity of which we already have argued for.[105]

---

[105] Gary R. Habermas and Michael Licona, *The Case for The Resurrection of Jesus*, Kregel Publications; First Edition, 2004,
Michael R. Licona, *The Resurrection of Jesus: A New Historiographical Approach*, InterVarsity Press, 2010,
N.T. Wright, "The Resurrection of Jesus", *Christian Origins and the Question of God*, Vol. 3, Fortress Press, 2003.

The first fact is that Jesus died on the cross. The Gospels attest that Jesus was sentenced to crucifixion and give many details as to how that went. We have extensive knowledge of what death by crucifixion means from the various documents about the practice of it found throughout the remains of the Roman Empire. We know that it involved being lashed repeatedly with a cat o' nine tail style whip with bits of bone and metal, designed to tear the flesh and expose both bones and internal organs. Crucifixion was performed by nailing a person to wooden cross at their wrists and ankles in such a way that if criminals sought to relieve pain from pressure on the wrists they could only push up on their ankles. If they wanted relief from the pain in their ankles, they could only hang from their wrists.

The usual cause of death in crucifixion is asphyxiation. The person is kept from breathing while futilely adjusting for the pain and dies for lack of air. In Palestine, the Romans adopted the custom of not allowing crucifixions to go past the Sabbath. They would hurry the death of the person by breaking their legs so they could no longer push up and die more quickly. It is clear that the operation would see to it that no one could live. However, the text indicates that the Roman Soldiers already found that Jesus was dead and shoved a spear into his side to make sure. The description of "blood and water" coming out suggests death by cardiovascular seizure leading to actual damage of the heart.

The actual nature of death by crucifixion is depicted with explicit detail in the movie "The Passion of the Christ" which seems to be part of the purpose of the film. Such a torturous death rules out the notion Jesus passed out or swooned but did not die on the cross. Even if, per improbable, that was the case, we could not expect a person so damaged being able to move the stone on his tomb or getting very far without being identified. That Jesus died on the cross is not often seriously questioned.

IV.   THE PLOT THINS: EMPTY TOMB

The second fact that points to the reality of the resurrection is the empty tomb. The tomb that Jesus was buried in was said to belong to Joseph of Arimathea, who was both a rich man and a member of the Sanhedrin, the ruling court of the Jews. If the disciples had wanted to make up a story it would not have been a good idea to pick the tomb of a prominent man in the community who might recognize himself and act against them. But such a man as Joseph would be well known and recognized. The text also indicates that the tomb was in a garden. Both the type of tomb, and the fact that it is in a garden, indicate that it would be the tomb of a rich man. In Jerusalem, there is a cemetery were such tombs are found in a garden next to the city gate, called the Garden Gate. There would be no mistaking the location of this tomb and no likelihood that anyone seeking the body of Jesus would go to the wrong tomb.

The historicity of the tomb story is attested by the reference to women in the Gospels, especially a woman with a bad reputation, as the first visitors to the tomb to see that it was empty. The testimony of women was, except in the case of special prominent cases, not recognized by the Jewish courts. So if the evidence were contrived it would not be likely to be attributed to a female eyewitness. Further, when the disciples began just seven weeks later to report Jesus as rising from the dead, the Jews could have easily reproduced the body and put a stop to it. Yet the story the Jewish leaders spread according to the New Testament was that the disciples stole the body, an exceedingly implausible story given that the tomb had an official Roman seal and was protected by Roman guards to prevent such a thing. Even this story attests to a common knowledge of an empty tomb. References to an empty tomb are conspicuous by their absence in the apostles' early preaching in Acts, which suggests that the empty tomb was a widely accepted detail that did not need to be mentioned. It seems very likely then that the grave in which the dead body of Jesus was laid was found empty.

V. NOT SO BEAUTIFUL MINDS: THE EYEWITNESS ACCOUNTS

The third fact substantiating the resurrection is that Jesus was seen alive and in the flesh by several witnesses. The New Testament reports several eyewitness accounts from various people. When Paul wrote in I Corinthians 15 that he appeared to a large mass of people, he mentions that several of them were still living and consultable at the time. Still it is often suggested that either the disciples were lying or hallucinating. But we can raise the same question about their motivations for lying as we did for Jesus earlier in this chapter. There was no rational profit that could be expected within a reasonable time frame and no reason to preserve the claim in the face of torture and death. So it is more often suggested that the disciples were hallucinating.

To appreciate what it means to hallucinate, we might recall the film "A Beautiful Mind" about the great economist and game theorist, John Nash. John Nash suffered from acute episodes of schizophrenia, including hallucinations of a CIA agent who had assigned him to read magazines to look for secret coded messages sent by Communist spies. Nash eventually learned how to cope with his hallucinations but they were with him his entire life. Nash's case illustrates many of the features of hallucinogenic episodes. They are either very short and occasional or lifelong. They do not disclose any new material but are only made of material already available to the mind that has them. They are strongly associated only with intimate and familiar places and they are private. There really is no such thing as group hallucinations. Hallucinations only form within a private point of view.

Compare Nash with the story from Luke of the disciples on the road to Emmaus.[106] This story happens right after a story where the women first come to the disciples to report the empty tomb and right before a story where these two return to the rest of the disciples to report seeing Jesus only to find that Jesus has already appeared to all of them "including Simon" who was not present in the first story. This indicates that the disciple named in the story was Luke's primary source for all three events, since he did not see the appearance of Jesus to the rest of the disciples but

---

[106] Luke 24.

was there for all three events. This attests to the historicity of the account, especially given the preface to the Gospel of Luke.

The disciples had noticed Jesus as a man walking ahead of them for a while but did not recognize who he was. This was experienced by both disciples as an ordinary experience of another person. Further, Jesus had explained from the Old Testament why these events had to take place, imparting new information and understanding, which they did not know before. Finally, Jesus physically interacted with the disciples by sitting with them and breaking their bread. This experience does not really compare to Nash's hallucinations. There are several reports of Jesus appearance where he teaches, eats, builds, and makes physical contact, with the disciples as a group. Finally, the disciples had several experiences of Christ but not lifelong ones.

Finally, if the disciples wanted to make up a life after death story they would be more likely to make up a story of transmigration like that of Enoch or Elijah in Jewish tradition. Though, there was an idea of bodily resurrection in Judaism at the time, it was rigidly associated with the last Judgment and not before. So it is unlikely that the appearances of Jesus alive after he died were hallucinations or deceptions.

VI.   THE UNPRECEDENTED COMMUNITY

The last fact which seems to prove the resurrection is that immediately after the death of Jesus a radically different community emerged among his followers that was unprecedented in either Judaism or Greek culture. It was never likely that the disciples would have any point in pressing on after the death of their leader. The disciples before the death of Christ clearly indicated that they believed that Jesus was the promised Messiah who would save Israel from Rome. They could not understand his references to dying in Jerusalem and were scattered at his death. Psychologically, they were utterly discouraged to see these hopes dashed. We are aware of how other Messianic claimants tried to rouse the crowd against Rome but nothing came of their movements after the leader was killed. Yet, suddenly Jesus' disciples began risking death and preaching the Gospel of peace, a radical transformation.

There would be no reasonable personal gain from such a movement. What they preached was considered blasphemous by all orthodox Jews. They would be upset by the changes made to the Old Testament Law, such as food laws and the day of the Sabbath. Nor would the Jews accept Jesus as God or a failed Messiah. Yet the disciples maintained their new convictions to the end of their lives. All but John were killed, and he was exiled. Furthermore, the church included converts who, when Jesus was alive, refused to accept him or his teachings, but who became leaders in the church, such as Paul and James, the brother of Jesus. This is especially important since no one could be an apostle if they could not show that they saw Jesus alive after death.

Before the days of sophisticated critical tools for doing history were developed, the Catholic Church could only point to its own existence as evidence of the resurrection. But there is still some truth to this. The church was unlikely to come into existence in the character that it did, but more likely to do so if the resurrection had occurred.

VII. CONCLUSION: INFERENCE AND NATURALISM

Taking these facts as established, they seem to be well explained by the simple claim that Jesus was raised bodily from the dead. This explanation, though marvelous, is most natural and simple, given these facts. It seems the only reason that one would have to reject this explanation for practically any other is a prior commitment to naturalism as a worldview. But if one does, one will have to explain why these facts appear to indicate a resurrection. Some have suggested a mass conspiracy to deceive the world. However, a conspiracy seems out of the question or at least extremely farfetched. Another explanation, that the church borrowed from the myths of resurrection in various cults and mystery religions, also seems farfetched. Such myths were used to explain the changing of the seasons and would not have likely found a good reception in Palestine.

We conclude that both the self-consciousness of Jesus and the resurrection of Jesus from the dead are the best explanations for these recalcitrant facts. They can only be resisted by a settled commitment to naturalism. An open minded agnostic might seriously consider adjusting his metaphysic to fit the facts better. It is possible that one could hold to the death and resurrection of the Jesus with a moral certainty.

Given that a resurrection is a genuine miracle, it indicates that God did and does endorse Jesus and his message. This includes endorsing Jesus' view of himself as the Son of Man as well as the unique Son of God. We also conclude that this is a divine endorsement of Jesus' claim to original authority as God. It seems likely that Jesus is an example that satisfies desiderata of a special act of God in our space and time history to reveal His good will to us. It remains to say that there is nothing like this in any of the other world religions. No religious leader claims to have the same central and essential status within their religion as Jesus does in the Apostolic tradition, nor do any of the legends about them have the same credible attestation that Jesus' life, death, and resurrection has. Jesus may reasonably claim to be God's only way of redemption.

16. The Book Where God Still Speaks

I. INTRODUCTION: VERBAL INSPIRATION

Having argued for the Resurrection of Jesus, we have thus also argued for the truth of Jesus' teaching. We take his claims about himself to be vouchsafed to us by God's miraculous hand. At this point in our reflections, to accept this as true would just be to accept that Jesus is the Lord and Christ, the Son of God. It would be to face the decision to become a Christian, just as those who first listened to Peter in Acts 2. But in addition to the authority of Christ, God provided a further source and authority, namely the Scriptures. In this chapter, we are going to examine the claim that the Scriptures are inspired to be God's own Word.

According to the Christian Church, human beings wrote the Scripture as they were inspired by God to write. This is the concept of verbal inspiration. What does this mean? This does not mean that the Scriptures were purely dictated. Although some Scriptures describe themselves as repeating God's word's after Him, we are not saying that the whole Scripture came from divine dictation. It also does not mean that inspiration is mechanistic. We do not hold that God used the authors as one might use a marionette, manipulating them so completely that their actions are not their own. Nor is inspiration meant to refer simply to God's general providential control over nature conceiving of the writing of Scripture as a part of providence. Such providence does not involve authority or infallibility, nor can it be said to give God's express will. Inspiration is the work of God, particularly the work of the Holy Spirit, seeing and overseeing the human author to such a degree that the author is led to produce words that are the very words of God. It is a fine grained providence that preserves the author's autonomy with respect to his own freedom, yet produces God's own words, so that the Scripture is both God's words and the human authors', without the human authors being used like a mere means. This doctrine is often illustrated by comparing it to the Incarnation, even though the synergy between God and man in inspiration does not involve the identification of God with the individual authors.

The possibility of inspiration is implied by the possibility of propositional revelation. All inspiration requires is that some revelation be propositional. True judgments per se are propositional so that being true is no obstacle to propositional expression. Nor is it impossible for God to accommodate His revelation to the capacity of His finite human creation's mind. As John Calvin has put it, God adapts to us as a human father uses baby talk to his infant child. The value of inspiration, if true, is considerable. It delivers reason from the dilemma of presuming to know the will of God by reason alone which is beyond our finite capacity or despairing of any knowledge of God's will whatsoever. Further, in the Scriptures, the saint has the very word of God from God. It is possible then for the believer to receive truth from God Himself immediately as if God is directly speaking to the believer. The tradition also holds that one's understanding of Scripture is made possible by the present active work of God in the Person of the Holy Spirit in illuminating the believer's reading of the text.

Thus the believer may encounter the Living God face to face in the text. The concept of propositional revelation therefore does not require that we reduce revelation to being mere expressions of our devotional feeling or a mirror of our own rational moral codes or some kind of final encounter that words cannot express when the Bible "becomes" the Word of God to us. Rather because God is personal and the cause of personality, we expect propositional revelation to adequately communicate with us.[107]

In arguing for inspiration, we accept what has been established so far; the possibility of knowledge, the existence of God, the Lordship of Jesus, and the historicity of the New Testament. We do not start from the presumption of inspiration to argue in a circle. Thus inspiration is the last thing we establish in apologetics, not the first.

II. PALESTINIAN JUDAISM, THE APOSTLES, AND CHRIST

In this section we will sum up what we know from both New Testament sources and external sources to show how we establish the inspiration of Scripture. It is clearly established is that verbal inspiration was what the Jews who lived in Jesus day claimed for the Old Testament writings. For them "Scripture says" and "God says" are interchangeable locutions. Even though the Old Testament books were authored like other human books they were also seen as if the words came from God's own hand.

---

[107] Ronald H. Nash, *The Word of God and the Mind of Man*, P&R Publishing, 1992.

The extent of God's assured inspiration extended not only to the words but even the parts of words and letters.[108]

It is also clear from the recognized writings of the Apostles of the early church, that the Apostles shared the same view of the Old Testament as the Jews did. In this, there was no change in doctrine from the Jewish community to the apostolic band in the view of Scripture. Scripture is said by Paul to be *theopnuesto* ("God breathed")[109] and the most likely meaning of this is the Jewish view. So the Jews and apostles held to verbal inspiration. But the apostles did break from the Jews in one respect on this. They applied the category of Scripture, not just to the Old Testament but also to each other's writings, Paul lumping selections from Luke with Old Testament references in citing Scripture[110] and Peter classifying Paul's writing with "other Scripture".[111] This indicates that they had the same view of the Apostles' writings as inspired as they did the prophetic writings.

With respect to the Old Testament, we see the Apostles attributing the same view of inspiration to Jesus as they held. Jesus expressly says about the Old Testament cannon recognized by the Jews of his day, "The Scripture cannot be broken" as a necessary truth always to be regarded. He says of the law that not one "jot or tittle" which are parts of Hebrew letters, shall pass away.[112] Jesus also says the same thing about his own original teaching

---

[108] B. B. Warfield, *The Inspiration and Authority of the Bible*, P & R Publishing; 2nd edition, 1980
[109] 2 Timothy 3:16.
[110] 1 Timothy 5:8, see Deuteronomy 25:4 and Luke 10:7.
[111] 2 Peter 3:16.
[112] Matthew 5:18.

("my words shall never pass away", "whoever listens to me is like the man who built his house on a rock"). Jesus claimed original authority for his teaching and the crowds recognized it.[113]

Jesus also commissioned the Apostles to continue to speak in his name and gave them His Holy Spirit to teach them many things they had yet to learn, things that they did not get from Jesus while alive, but are on par with the authority Jesus had for his own original teaching.[114] The special blessing of the Holy Spirit was an endorsement of the authority of the Apostles. Such an authority could extend to their writings and seems to have done so. It seems clear that the apostles did not think that everything they said was to be taken with inspired authority just as was apparently true about the prophets in the Old Testament. Only when the Apostles were speaking by the Holy Spirit did their words have divine authority.

To sum up, whatever was written by the Prophets when they claimed divine authority is taken to be divine authority by Jesus. Similarly, whatever was written by the Apostles when they claimed to be speaking from the Lord or by the Spirit has divine authority based on the commission of Jesus to the Apostles. Jesus has divine authority for us based on the attestation to his message by his character and God's miracles. And so we take the writings of the Old and New Testament as divinely authorized and inspired since written by the prophets and Apostles. Because of the authority of Jesus, we accept biblical inspiration.

---

[113] Mark 13:31, Matthew 24:35, Luke 21:33.
[114] John 16:7-15.

III. ALTERNATIVE HYPOTHESES

But before we do, we need to consider alternative explanations that have been offered for the status of the biblical writings. One common suggestion is that while it is certainly true that the Jews and Apostles held to verbal inspiration, Jesus, the original theological genius he must have been, did not. The language in which it appears that he does is essentially only in ad hominem arguments against the Pharisees, such as "If you do believe that the Scripture is infallible and that these writings are Scripture, then you would do such and such".[115] They are thus not an actual claim to endorse the doctrine of verbal inspiration.

However, the view seems to involve a double standard concerning evidence, because while certain evidence for the Apostles' view is said to prove they held verbal inspiration, similar evidence concerning Jesus is explained away or dismissed. The Sermon on the Mount[116] is presented as evidence that he corrected Scripture and thus did not share the Jewish view of Scripture. But we venture to suggest that a closer reading of that text will show that rather correcting the Scripture text, Jesus is supplementing it with words based on his own parity of authority with it. At any rate, such a view fails to isolate Jesus' view from the Apostles since the Apostles preached this view on Jesus imprimatur of authority as we saw.[117]

---

[115] John 5:46,47.
[116] Matthew 5-7, See especially Chapter 5.
[117] Stuart C. Hackett, *The Reconstruction of Christian Revelation Claim.*

Another hypothesis is that Jesus' remarks about Scripture are a form of missionary accommodation, or a contextual adaptation. Jesus adopted the cultural viewpoint on Scripture "to be all things to all men" but he did not hold it himself, only attributing his authority to the certain passages used by him. But this defies the logic of the arguments Jesus' use Scripture, appealing to the claim that Scripture being Scripture cannot be broken. At any rate, Jesus must have failed to see to it that his true view was passed on to the disciples, nor do we have evidence of an alternate view in the teaching of Jesus. But worst of all, no one can stand to attribute such a view of accommodation to the morally upright Jesus, because it involves creating and perpetuating a distinctly false impression in order to be accepted, and argues that the ends justify the means. For all of the reasons we gave concerning Jesus' character in chapter 15, we should not expect this to be true.

Some, feeling the bite of this last point, want to simply say that there was no malfeasance involved. It was simply that Jesus or the Apostles believed the Jewish doctrine out of ignorance and followed along with the crowd. This seems to make it a rule that whatever is said that is like what is said by others has no authority. But this rule seems to prove too much. It entails that much we would paradigmatically expect to be authoritative is not so, such as the commandment to "Do unto others as you would have others do unto you". The impact of the rule is to make most of the New Testament teaching nothing but waste.

Another view is based on the point made earlier that not all the apostles did or said is meant to count as authoritative teaching. It reduces what does so count by requiring that only those points that the Apostles explicitly introduced as doctrine have Christ's authority. Inspiration is not one of them. However, most traditional doctrine taken from the Old and New Testament also fails this test. Furthermore, the results of this test bring us again back to a certain smaller set of proof texts which are the measure of all doctrine, and ironically bring back a kind of fundamentalism. It is evident from the apostolic writings that the theological content of the Scripture is much more holistic and thematic and not expressed by some bullet point doctrinal statements. To accept this view is to back away from the progress scholars have made in Biblical theology.

Another approach is the view that whatever the doctrine of inspiration means has to be determined by the phenomena of Scripture. According to this view, we need to make an accounting of the observable text with all of its puzzling difficulties and proportion the sense of inspiration to the results. One is tempted ask, given such a method, how could we know if the doctrine of inspiration is true. This is similar to the view of natural laws we saw earlier that said that they are just the descriptions of what we regularly observe in nature, thus methodologically ruling out the possibility of a miracle suspending natural law. By parity of reasoning, we would have to identify Aristotle's doctrine of the Soul with whatever the assured results of behavioral studies would be, and attribute to the meaning of Darwin's theory of natural selection whatever the outcome of research in natural history research may be. But it is clear that we are able to identify, and thus evaluate, what these men meant by the soul and the process of evolution by an examination of their expositions.

Similarly, we can know what Jesus and the Apostles meant by inspiration from what they say and how they use the Scriptures before examining the whole phenomena of the text. Thus we may verify, confirm, or falsify their theory by the text. Furthermore equating the meaning of inspiration with just the results of investigation obscures the force of the distinction between apparent difficulties and real errors. It would not be possible for the Apostles to be found wrong in their view since their view is just whatever the phenomena tells us.

But a common feature of all these alternative hypotheses is that if we take them to be true, then we must reject the claim that Jesus had any integrity or competence since it was Jesus who was responsible for bestowing his authority on despicable or incompetent transmitters of his teaching and did so either ignorantly or deceitfully. And thus Jesus could not be the Lord he said he was which would make Christianity false. Thus the actual displayed and recorded character and competence of Jesus counts against the reasonableness of these theories.

IV. INSPIRATION, INFALLIBILITY, AND INERRANCY

So we are arguing that the best explanation of the evidence is that the Apostles affirmed verbal inspiration and did so with the authority granted them by Jesus Christ, and thus that verbal inspiration is true. If so, then the Bible is the word of God and is thus infallible, since God cannot fail. Does this mean then that the Bible is inerrant?

The claim to Biblical inerrancy is one that stirs up all kinds of terrible impressions. Linguistically, it seems associated with an idealistic theory of language that treats the Bible as a list of assertions about all topics that are open to verification. Interpretatively, it suggests that the only proper way to understand the text in all circumstances is literally. This view of the Bible is false and untenable, as it would be as a view of literature in general.

In order to understand the concepts of infallibility and inerrancy, we need to take a brief look at the philosophy of language. There have been attempts to reform language itself so as to remove its poly-functional character and its ambiguities. But the limited results from this revisionist project have led many linguists to see their first job as just describing the way language is actually used, assuming that language is fine the way it is. Many have gone even farther and come to minimize any truth telling or asserting function to language, seeing various language practices as pointing to nothing outside themselves.[118]

A middle and better approach to language that respects the diversity of function and the capacity for truth telling is called "speech act theory".[119] On this view, in ordinary situations language use is a form of action. We do things with words. Like other actions, a speaker's speech can be analyzed by the various ways it aims to achieve its goals. Consider someone yelling

---

[118] Ludwig Wittgenstein, *Philosophical Investigations,* Prentice Hall; 3rd edition, 1973.
[119] John R. Searle, *Speech Acts: An Essay on the Philosophy of Language*, Cambridge University Press, 1970.

"Fire!" in crowded theater. He is doing four things according to speech act theory. First, he is making the oral utterance "Fire!" very loudly. This is how he says what he wants to say. Second, he is saying that there is a fire in the theatre. This is the full locutionary act he wants to accomplish by urgently saying "Fire!" Third, by saying this, he is thereby warning the audience there is a fire. This is the illocutionary act of what is being said. Finally, there is an intended result, namely to get the audience to move out of the theatre for their own safety, called the perlocutionary act. Every speech act can be analyzed into these four aspects.

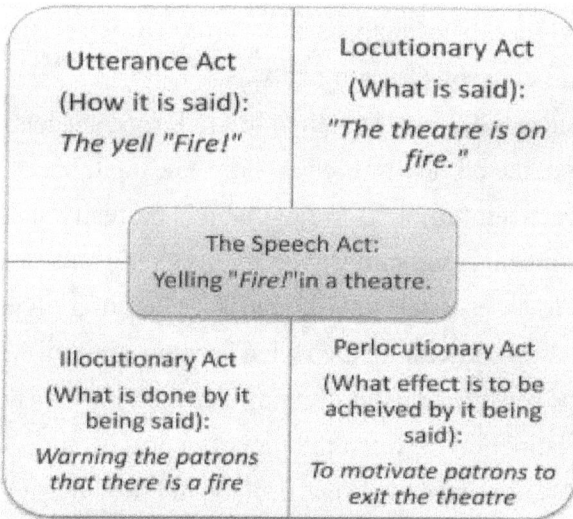

Figure 1: Speech Act Analysis Example

To say that the Bible is God's Word is to say that the Bible contains God's speech acts. As the speech acts of God, they cannot fail in their purposes and aims. This includes each of these four aspects. Speech act theory illuminates the various ways the same illocutionary act can be accomplished by differing locutionary acts, or how the same locutionary act can be realized by different utterance acts, and so on. We can use speech act theory to shed light on how metaphors (e.g. "the fog came in on little cat feet") work differently from plain prose. They work by making the same locutionary acts but different utterance and illocutionary acts from prose statements. And we can explain how phenomenal or approximate language can be used to make assertions (e.g "the sun will rise at 6 o'clock") by making the same locutionary acts but different utterance and perlocutionary acts. Also speech act analysis is not arbitrary or a matter of taste. We can give reasons for our analysis.

Since the Bible is taken to be God's speech acts by divine inspiration, the biblical speech acts must be infallible. To say that a speech act is infallible is to say that it is perfectly successful in coordinating all its functions with the speaker's intentions. When it comes to cases where the illocutionary act of a divine speech act is to assert something, then what is being asserted will be true. That is the sense that inspiration implies inerrancy. In making the natural distinction between the illocutionary act, the locutionary act, and the utterance act, we affirm that there is inerrant propositional truth in the Scriptures, but we neither insist on a literal interpretation of the Scriptures nor claim that all the Scripture does assert things.

V. TEXTUAL AND CANONICAL CRITICISM

Of course, verbal inspiration does not settle the question of what books and materials are Scriptural. What we have is that if something is Scripture then it is inspired. But what is Scripture and what isn't?

First, what is Scripture in terms of which books are part of the canon, the list of texts the church accepts as Scripture? The process of canonization took place for both testaments over periods of time when people were appropriately acquainted with the original authors or their disciples or schools, including their oral traditions and written commentary. There were also responsible witnesses to the provenance, distribution, and use of the books within the history of the communities. In all this, it seems clear that the requirement for recognition as canon is that the book had a prophetic or apostolic approved source. In each case, there were paradigm examples of accepted work, but also some disputed cases (Esther, Maccabees, Revelation, Hermas). Eventually the church was able to achieve an appropriate confidence on the canon.[120]

The Church's recognition of the canon is not the source of our recognition since that recognition had to be based on the indications of appropriate authority. This means that the set of Scripture is a bit fuzzy relative to us, an errant collection of inerrant books. However, this judgment obscures the different degrees of legitimate confidence we can have in the books in our canon. Comparing what is clear in its authority with what is not so much so, we see that no doctrine essential to Christianity is

---

[120] F.F. Bruce, *The Canon of Scripture*, IVP Academic, 1988.

affected by this and that in fact many other doctrines are well established.

Once we settle which books are canonical, the next question is the text. Inspiration applies to the original writing of the documents. This presents a problem because none of the original documents have survived. What is the use of inspired but non-existing documents? But as we have seen in chapter 14, the textual resources for the New Testament are very good. In the case of the Old Testament, most of our extant sources of Old Testament writing go only as far back as about the ninth century, until the discovery of the Dead Sea Scrolls which predate the events of the New Testament. They show that there has been a remarkable preservation of the Old Testament text from that day until now. We also know about the ancient specific practices of the Jewish community that saw to the preservation of the Old Testament text. These also assure us of the reliable textual transmission. Finally, it was the Dead Sea era textual and canonical process from the Dead Sea Scroll date forward that Jesus accepted.

Applying the doctrine of inspiration here, the result was not only an inspired original specific manuscript but an inspired text transmitted. Just as we have this same text in several different printed copies, we have the same text as the original inspired manuscripts in all of its copies. So we still have the inspired text today that the Apostles gave us. But it lies among the many alternative text manuscripts and other artifacts. So we must use textual criticism to reconstruct the most likely account of the original text. Furthermore, textual criticism, unlike speculative "higher criticism", is based on a common sense form of reasoning with some clear criteria. The only question the text critic asks is the typically answerable question of whether this manuscript or that one is most likely the original text. It does not ask the more speculative and opaque question of what we should expect the text to most likely say, nor is it necessary to do so. Like the question of canonicity, this means the boundaries of Scripture are a bit vague to us. But again most of the text is reliably constructed and what is in dispute is not significant in its effect on the teaching of the Bible. The body of reliable Scripture is very thick in proportion to its size, and the fuzzy boundary of it is very thin. The evidence is consistent with the claim that God has seen to it that His Word has been transmitted through the centuries.

VI. THE PHENOMENA OF SCRIPTURE

Returning to the question of the relation between the doctrine of inspiration and the phenomena of Scripture, we have given reason for accepting the doctrine based on the authority of Christ and independently from looking at the text. In dealing with difficult and puzzling problems and apparent discrepancies amongst the phenomena of Scripture, whether from science or history, or from numberings or dates, or New Testament use of the Septuagint, or anything else, our argument implies a strong prior plausibility for the fact of inspiration over against these problems. We are entitled to be a bit obstinate in the face of apparent difficulties.[121]

We can compare the situation of inspiration with some themes from the philosophy of science. Imre Lakatos is a philosopher and a scientific realist we considered in Chapter 4. As we saw, he observed that scientific statements could not simply be identified as either being observational statements or theoretical statements. In real life, scientific theorizing usually involves sets of statements logically interwoven with one another. It is not the individual statements in isolation that are supported or disconfirmed by evidence but rather the whole network of statements in a research program taken together. Further, he argued that evidence did not simply prove or refute these sets of statements but rather the total set of theories adjusted to the whole body of evidence. If such adjustments could not be made in an effective way, then a scientist would consider rejecting the whole for another research thesis.[122]

According to Lakatos, a research program with its set of received theories could be characterized like a snowball. At the icy center is a hard core of assumptions and definitions that are held fixed throughout the research. They function as the gatekeepers for what is and what is not accepted into the program. Around them is a solidified layer of theories and claims that have great weight but which remain open to minor adjustments in the light of new evidence. The expectation is that these theories have

---

[121] C.S. Lewis, "On Obstinancy of Belief", *The World's Last Night and Other Essays*, Mariner Books, 2002.
[122] Brendon Larvor, *Lakatos: An Introduction*.

already been well confirmed and that new evidence will confirm them more. In the outermost powder-like surface are the theories that are most affected by the evidence. They are made to deal with difficulties the program raises and in part contain pastiche theories or ad hoc hypotheses that do not satisfactorily deal with the problems. They do allow the program to continue in the hope that eventually these problems will be solved in light of further research. If the program as a whole is surviving tests without too much accommodation, scientists are more inclined to hold onto it into the future, and Lakatos argues that they are rational to do so.

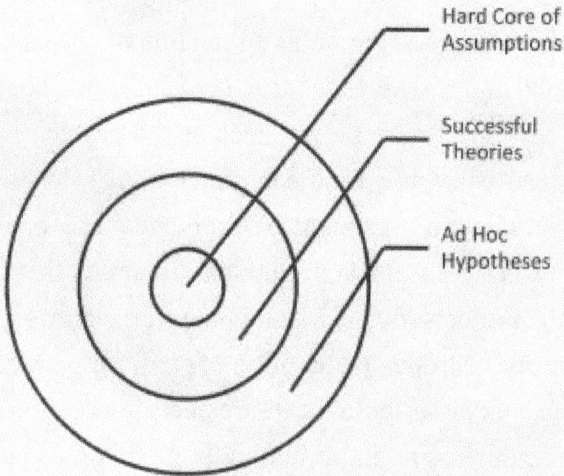

Figure 2: Imre Lakatos' Research Program "Snowball"

The same may be applied to the study of the Bible as Scripture. In that case, the doctrine of verbal inspiration provides the hard core assumption of exegesis, the middle band the viable interpretations of the text from previous exegesis and theological research that are successful and coherent, and the outer band are the proposed solutions to the difficulties raised by internal tensions among the text or external tensions between the text and history or natural science or the transmission of individual texts and what not. As long as the study of Scripture is a flourishing program and is not swallowed up by the outer band, the reasonableness of inspiration remains well attested.

When we think of the matter this way, it seems that the number of difficulties or their nature has not yet made them so onerous to threaten the project. Archeology has done much to reduce the number of them. Even the tide of critical studies has contributed much to assuage the list of problems. There certainly have been some strong blows, such as the problems created by geology and astronomy for the interpretation of Genesis, but there is no overwhelming cataract of problems. The one important difference between this and Lakatos' picture is that our chosen hard core is not stipulated but is a prior claim supported by evidence and a strong presumption of credibility. Also since this picture encompasses both Scripture and science, this means that we take science as an important external criteria of interpreting Scripture and vice versa, since both are mutually adjusting programs to new facts. Scripture is infallible but all truth is God's truth.

In this context, it is helpful to think of the story of the resistance fighter that we used in Chapter 7. The French Resistance Leader makes such an impression that the fighters are willing to give him the benefit of the doubt when it seems like he's leading the enemy to victory. This doesn't mean there are no conceivable circumstances where the fighters will finally conclude that he's betrayed them, just that such circumstances cannot be made explicit in advance.

VII. THE COHERENCE OF SCRIPTURE

When it comes to the interpretation of the Bible as Scripture, we find that there is much that does indicate a flourishing project. The Scriptures of the Old and New Testament display a striking degree of coherence. By coherence, we do not mean a mere lack of contradictory assertions, nor the coherence of a deductive system like Euclidian geometry. The internal coherence of Scripture, as Dr. Stuart Cornelius Hackett describes it, is like the coherence of a human life from childhood to adulthood.[123] What was all mystery becomes more intelligible as more is revealed over the course of time, from fullness to fullness. Furthermore, the Scripture is characterized by coherence in relation to the world around it. The message of Scripture makes sense of the strange dualities, such as between personality and communication and a world of physical processes, human greatness and fragileness, and human dignity and depravity. Further,

---

[123] Hackett, *The Reconstruction of Christian Revelation Claim.*

Scripture answers the questions of where we came from, where we are going, and why. The various departments of knowledge and spheres of life are brought into unity by the basic schema of Scripture: Creation, Fall, Redemption, and Consummation. Finally we can say of Scripture what essayist G. K. Chesterton says of the Church, namely that it not only has taught but continues to teach even to us today.[124]

Such coherence does not rule out paradoxes but rather expects them, given that the claim is that the Bible is God's own self-disclosure. In the Bible, and in the theology seeking to grasp and express the truth in the Bible, we find many cases of apparent contradictions, such as divine predestination and human responsibility, nature and grace, creation and supernatural action, the dignity and depravity of human beings, divine goodness and divine severity, the kingdom that is already here but also not yet here, as well as the doctrine of one God and yet three Divine Persons, Father, Son, and Spirit, the doctrine of verbal inspiration, the doctrine of the incarnation of God in Man, the doctrines of substitutionary atonement, Christ died in our place, and imputed righteousness, we declared righteous though still sinners. And so on.

Yet the theologian is in a similar situation to the scientist, especially the scientist who studies theoretical physics and cosmology. The physicist is also in a position where he or she is reduced to formulating theories with a similar paradoxical nature

---

[124] Geerhardus Vos, *Biblical Theology*, Banner of Truth, 1975,
Brian Walsh and J. Richard Middleton, *The Transforming Vision: Shaping a Christian Worldview*, IVP Academic, 1984.

such as particle/wave duality of force fields, the Heisenberg Uncertainty Principle, and the tension between general relativity and quantum physics. The logic of these formulations does not provide a full explanation of the fundamental realities, yet the results of the observations require and constrain the character of the description. It does not imply that anything follows from these paradoxes as we would expect in the case a mere contradiction. That is because the picture is controlled by observational and other theoretically established constraints. Rather than being a pure theory, these formulas are rather successful models of the phenomena which we do not yet fully understand.

The case is similar with revelation. Many features seem paradoxical, but they are constrained by the data of Scripture. Biblical doctrines are neither necessarily a perfect theoretical system nor are they totally imperspicuous and devoid of content. They cannot be asserted or combined willy nilly and not just anything follows from them. They can be said to picture the content of God's revelation revealed in Scripture. This is not surprising if Scripture is God adapting what he wants humans to know to their finite capacities. Revelation does not try to fit God into the human mind but TO open the mind to behold God. Such paradoxes count as much against the coherence of biblical revelation as the paradoxes of physics count against the coherence of science.[125]

---

[125] E. L. Mascal, *Existence and Analogy*, Darton, Longman, & Todd Ltd; New impression edition, 1966,
Ian T. Ramsey, *Models and Mystery*, Oxford University Press, 1964.

All these features of the text point to an identifiable and intelligible unity that transcends the diverse features one recognizes in the individual authors and their sources, as well as a mystery that can substantially but not fully appreciated by the human mind. One may notice a critical mass of internal evidence of the Mind of one Author behind such diversity and not only its unity but also its character. In this sense, we see that the phenomena of Scripture may even bear witness to its own divine origin and confirm the testimony of Christ to its inspiration. We invite readers to see for themselves.

VIII. CONCLUSION: THEOLOGY AS SCIENCE AND THE BOOK

Returning now to the beginning of our investigation, we have been arguing that Christianity is knowledge. We argued that in any science there has to be an object to know, a subject that may know it, and a means by which the object may become known by the subject. And now we have argued that by this definition, theology is a science. We have argued that its Object, God, exists, that man in his nature points to God, and that God has in creation, and may have in history, made himself known to man. Then we further argued that that this has indeed happened in the person of Jesus Christ and in providing the Bible as God's self-revelation in His Word. Having established this much, we only add that it is from these sources that the whole of the Gospel and Christian Doctrine are based and by the authority of which it receives its truth. Thus, by our argument, we have provided a reason to believe that Christianity is true.

Francis Schaeffer once told a story about a book that had all of its pages torn out. The shreds were scattered. Looking at them, it was difficult to make sense of them. But once the book binding was found, the page portions left at the binding made it possible to restore the book whole. But as Schaeffer points out, there still remains the task of reading the book. As Schaeffer puts it, we begin with reason but we finish with the whole person. Now that reason has brought to us the story of Christianity, we must take up and read. The final test is the pragmatic one, where we confirm the truth by seeing how it becomes confirmed in our own lives as we live by the promises of God.

Conclusion: Defense and Proclamation

We have come to the end of our little introduction in apologetics. We have ambitiously tried not only to make Christian claims seem plausible but even to show how theology satisfies the qualifications of being a science, including Christian theology. Christianity is both true and a source of truth. However, though we have stressed truth and science and objective inquiry, we also want to argue at the end that Christianity is also subjectively, practically, and personally true. There is a theology for the mind and a theology for the heart.

I. KNOWLEDGE AND NEWS

Walker Percy tells a story about a castaway on an island who, while walking on the beach, discovers several bottles each containing a piece paper with something written on it. Collecting them all and sorting them out, he discovers that some papers say things like "Boston is the capital of Massachusetts", "The ratio of the circumference to the diameter of a circle is constant", and "Water molecules contain two hydrogen atoms and one oxygen atom". These statements are simply true or false. However, there are other papers that say things like "There is fresh water in the next cove", "The island is about to be attacked by pirates", and "Jill just had twins". Percy expects that even though these are like the others in seeming to report facts, they are significantly different because they deal with matters that are personally relevant to the castaway. The first type of statement is scientific. But the second type of statement is news. [126]

There are important differences between science and news. Science is detached from any personal relevance and is expressed *sub species aeternae*, from the perspective of the absolute. It invites further contemplation, speculation, and inquiry, but no action. Science is organized by an absolute hierarchy intrinsic to the facts. Science has to meet a strict and demanding standard of evidence, and scientific statements are evaluated according to the degree of confidence that is justified. News, however, is not ordered absolutely but ordered to the degree of importance it has for the person hearing it. News provokes not contemplation but a practical response. We think about science, but we act on news. Finally, news is accepted on a much more liberal standard than science. We verify science but we triage news. We are willing to gamble on a plausible news item if we are confident enough in the source and something urgent is at stake.

It is important to realize that while theology is a science, Christianity comes to us first and foremost as a proclamation. The Gospel is good news before it is science.

We estimate the evidential support for scientific theories and judge which are better supported than others or which are demonstrated and which have been shown to be false. These decisions do not entail commitments of our life and time. But we

---

[126] Walker Percy, *The Message in the Bottle: How Queer Man is, How Queer Language is, and What One Has to Do with the Other*, Picador; 1st Picador edition, 2000.

do decide to act on news and not necessarily until after we have all the facts. The criteria that we use to determine whether to accept a news story are; (a) whether or not we have any reason to dismiss the story out of hand as being contrary to known fact or incoherent, (b) whether or not the person bringing the news earns our trust, and (c) whether the relevance of news is urgent or important to us within our order of priorities. Science demands confirmation or falsification rather than mere lack of implausibility, the facts must stand on their own merits and not depend on the source, and it does not matter to science what relevance the truth may have for any particular person. Acting on news is not doing science, but it would be unreasonable to call irrational or irresponsible anyone who acted on news if these conditions were satisfied.

II. THE RATIONALITY CONDITION

In the first part of our study, we discovered that for many Christianity is already implausible because of the modern secular worldview of scientism, naturalism, and creative relativism. On such a view, Christianity is ruled out as if it violated some matter of fact or standard of logic. We also diagnosed the ubiquity of this view by an institutional analysis to show how it could be widely held without evidence. We then dealt with the some of the specific objections that try to show how Christianity fails to be coherent and consistent with the known facts and found them to be insufficient. But we did not stop there. Throughout nature, we have "God-signs".

In the second part, we made a positive case for theism, arguing that theology meets the necessary and sufficient conditions for being a science in the wider sense of being an objective inquiry. We gave several arguments for the existence of God and humanity's fitness to know God. At the same time we questioned whether the combination of scientism and skepticism and a commitment to metaphysical naturalism was coherent and non-arbitrary. Not only that but we have argued that the theistic worldview makes plausible the possibility of further revelation from God. We then also argued that the best explanation could be that God indeed has revealed Himself in Jesus Christ and even may speak to us in the Scriptures.

Most importantly, in defending Christian theology as a science, we have shown that it is well within the constraints of (a), the rationality condition. Secular society stands confidently on the presumed authority of a naturalistic worldview but there is no "money in the bank" that justifies this, only sophisticated intimidation.

III. THE CREDIBLITY CONDITION

As for (b), the credibility condition, we argued that even without supposing that the New Testament was infallible, it was still sufficient to put together a reliable biography of significant features of Jesus and the Apostles. It is possible to identify Jesus himself through his Apostles as the original source of the Christian message. From the same documents we can see that Jesus was an extraordinary man who was willing to die for his teachings. The Apostles too faced suffering and death for holding to the teaching of Jesus. The witness of the early church even after the period covered by the New Testament continues to show the marks of self-sacrifice and seriousness we see in the Apostles. While the current expression of the Church in the West may be said to be full of hypocrites, the Church that gave us the Gospel from within Palestine in the first century should impress us with its credibility. We may even say, since the credibility requirement does not necessarily require exemplary character, just that we have sufficient reason to trust a person's testimony given the circumstances, that we have a surplus of credibility, in the sources of the Gospel message.

IV. THE RELEVANCE CONDITION

Here and there, we have discussed various ways humanity itself enters the picture. We discussed that humans are disposed to God by nature, first in their restless pursuit of science and understanding, but also in their desire for truth and meaning. We discussed the odd situation described by Psalm 8, in which man is described as belonging to two frameworks. There is the cold empty realm of nature and the vastness of space, subject to the blind mechanisms of the natural laws, which will eventually wash away not only the individual but also the species and which moves determinedly to ultimate death. Human life is just a span in a potentially infinite history of nothingness.

Yet in spite of rising out of the mud, humans have a striking capacity to think and to understand the universe and to

299

manage it with technology, to detect values and order actions to goals, and to create beauty. Humans are not just aware of nature as a "thing", but also a hierarchy of "presences", from the most rudimentary cells to plants animals and each other. We are a "little lower than the angels".

One may accept these two perspectives and build an insightful tradition of natural religion. One may deny both as illusions in order to live exclusively in a subjective realm. Or one may reject one and keep the other as naturalism does, in order to attain a neutral and god-like stance over the world and to extinguish -- as if it were possible – the naturalist's own subjectivity and personhood. These are all ways of filling the time while the fundamental mystery of who we are remains untouched.

However, we also saw that alongside this is the voice of conscience that speaks to us in our soul. If God exists, we can see that this is God's voice calling us to account, not only in our mind but also in our experience and feelings. Conscience points to our responsibility but also to our moral failures. It does not, however, point to any ultimate solution to them. Further, we also saw that there is a persistent human tendency that works against character so that we do not want to identify with our actions. The behavior of those who reject God may be because they cannot bear the anxiety about their human situation or the wrestling with the guilt of their character. Better not to believe in God than go through dealing with trying to find peace with God.

It is important to see that Christianity is not just applied philosophical theology but rather revelation that came from the special initiative of God to bring about a new state of affairs into history. The Gospel is not knowledge about what is in nature but news from beyond nature that answers to man's strangeness as a dweller in two worlds. Further, the Gospel message is also addressed to human conscience and the problem of guilt before an ultimate Judge. This revelation finally culminates in a genuine word of God to us in the Scriptures.

If we read what the Apostles' tell us on Christ's authority , we see that the good news is that God the Judge has become God the Savior.

→ God has created the world and human beings for it. He has left signs of Himself in the world, of his greatness and his severity, including especially human beings as signs of God in their nature. He has also not left humanity without a witness about the ethical. Our responsibilities speak to us as a moral law through the conscience.

→ Yet though God is there, humans have become separated from Him and become all alone in the universe. This is connected with what our conscience tells us about our moral failings not just toward each other but toward Him in failing to acknowledge Him. Rather than seeking God, we have sought to make the world more to our own liking through religion and philosophy, replacing God with lesser goods. This not only broke our relationship to God, it left us unable to do anything to help ourselves from our sin and isolation.

→ But now God has taken the initiative to call humans back by sending his own Son, Jesus, as a human being to live righteously and then suffer and die like a criminal. Then to show

His acceptance of Jesus offering of his life, He raised Jesus from the death and made Him Lord of all. This is not a legendary story but an action of God which He performed in our space and time, and which has left clear traces in history.

→ Jesus laid the foundation for the Apostles and, through them, the Church to spread the good news to all nations that God had redeemed human beings so that whosoever will may be saved, be reconciled to God, and be reborn with a new power for living.

→ Now anyone may return to God through the Lord Jesus who recognize and loathe their own sin and turn away from their sin and trust in the work of redemption that the Lord Jesus achieved in his death and resurrection. Those that do become members of Jesus and part of his earthly mission to call all people to himself, until he comes back again as he promised. Those who refuse the gospel to serve their interests in the goods of this world will continue until the end to enjoy what they may. But after that there is no other opportunity for redemption other than the one they turned down.

In relation to Jesus then we now have peace with God when we acknowledge our sinfulness and turn from it to accept Jesus as our Savior and King. In this message, man's question is answered: "Where can I find God and find Him gracious?"

To anyone who finds that the human predicament we described applies to him or her, the message of a radically new state of affairs in the universe that restores life to lost human beings must not only be relevant but radically so. It is not simply knowledge of God nor news of the universe, but news from God for us.

V. THE LAST ARGUMENT

When Jesus came, according to the New Testament, to announce the good news of the arrival of his new Kingdom, he attested to his authority in life by casting out demons, and healing and feeding many. These miracles were, like his resurrection, signs of his authority on earth and the authority of his proclamation. These signs were miracles but they were also fitted to the mission by being gifts. They delivered people from enslaving powers like demons. They also sustained people by providing for their needs as God had done for Israel in the wilderness. Thus, they combined accreditation, real deliverance, real power, real justice, and real satisfaction.

Before Jesus left he appointed the Apostles to continue the mission that God had begun in him. He gave them the power to perform miracles in his name, even greater ones than his in his own earthly ministry. The Apostles were given yet more revelation as Jesus had promised and thus needed more confirmation by signs until the revelation given was that sufficient for the age. They created a community of faith, the church, for all those who trusted in the promise of God, to continue the mission of proclamation throughout the world until the end of the age.

Though the time of miracles is over for the moment, the saving power of God is still supposed to be manifest in the church. The Gospel is supposed to be the announcement of a new power of living, demonstrated in the love each Christian has for one another and for those who are outside. This must be at least substantially realized and palpable to strangers even though some sins remain until the consummation at the return of Jesus.

And so this is our last argument for Christianity. The church exists to proclaim this good news but it also must continue to fulfill her role as a sign. The church must be the miracle for today that confirms the truth of the message. Consequently, the church must be a community characterized by unity and love as well as holiness and truth. It must carry out Jesus' ministry of deliverance and mercy to all those who seek it from Jesus Christ. It is to confirm the truth of her proclamation by displaying the transforming power of the new life promised in the Gospel. This is also what Jesus calls us to do. Those who refuse to seek this display of transformation are disobedient to him and cannot be said to be his followers.[127]

This evidence is anecdotal but still necessary. Jesus has not insulated his church from pretenders who use Christianity as a pretext either to introduce their own novelties or as an excuse for any kind of behavior, even otherwise noble behavior. Such counterfeit Christianity should concern us precisely because it profanes the name and reputation of Jesus. But because Jesus himself has set the cost of discipleship very high, including giving up our lives for the sake of the gospel, those outside must base their judgment on the life of those who take the cost seriously and responsibly. This does not make the test trivial, because

---

[127] Francis Schaeffer, *The Mark of the Christian*, InterVarsity Press, 1984.

who can fulfill the cost of discipleship except those who know the transformative power of God?

But the church is not called to wait until the world finds her. She needs to go display herself before the watching world just as Jesus did. Christian apologetics is not just something the church does, but something the church is. As the classic biblical text that calls each Christian to be prepared to make a defense makes clear, both the doing and the being cannot be separated and neither can be neglected.

"Now who is there to harm you if you are zealous for what is good? But even if you should suffer for righteousness' sake, you will be blessed. Have no fear of them, nor be troubled, but in your hearts honor Christ the Lord as holy, always being prepared to make a defense to anyone who asks you for a reason for the hope that is in you; yet do it with gentleness and respect, having a good conscience, so that, when you are slandered, those who revile your good behavior in Christ may be put to shame. For it is better to suffer for doing good, if that should be God's will, than for doing evil."[128]

---

[128] 1 Peter 3:13 – 17, New Testament, English Standard Version, Crossway, 2006.

About the Author

John G. Hartung was born in Los Angeles, California and has lived in Nevada, Georgia, and Mississippi. He currently lives in Syracuse, New York. He served in the United States Air Force. He has a B. A. in Biblical Studies from Belhaven University, an M. Div. from Reformed Theological Seminary in Jackson, Mississippi, And an M. A. in philosophy from the University of Mississippi. He is an adjunct instructor at Le Moyne College and worships and serves with Trinity Fellowship Church (CCCC). He blogs at "The Gnuvenberist" at www.thegnijgh.wordpress.com. You can follow him on Twitter (@The_Gnu_JGH).

www.ingramcontent.com/pod-product-compliance
Lightning Source LLC
LaVergne TN
LVHW051454080426
835509LV00017B/1761